T0348256

# HOW TO BUILD A BUSINESS OTHERS WANT TO BUY

# HOW TO BUILD A BUSINESS

## KOBI SIMMAT

# OTHERS WANT TO BUY

WILEY

First published in 2023 by John Wiley & Sons Australia, Ltd
Level 4, 600 Bourke St, Melbourne Victoria 3000, Australia

Typeset in Palatino LT Std 10.5pt/15pt

© John Wiley & Sons Australia, Ltd 2023

The moral rights of the author have been asserted

ISBN: 978-1-394-19460-5

 A catalogue record for this book is available from the National Library of Australia

Cover design by Wiley
Figure 14.1: Notebook image: © Ananieva Elena/Shutterstock

**Disclaimer**
The material in this publication is of the nature of general comment only, and does not represent professional advice. It is not intended to provide specific guidance for particular circumstances and it should not be relied on as the basis for any decision to take action or not take action on any matter which it covers. Readers should obtain professional advice where appropriate, before making any such decision. To the maximum extent permitted by law, the author and publisher disclaim all responsibility and liability to any person, arising directly or indirectly from any person taking or not taking action based on the information in this publication.

Printed in Singapore
M125114A_250523

# TABLE OF CONTENTS

# ACKNOWLEDGEMENTS

This book is dedicated to everyone who has helped me along my journey to this incredible milestone.

To my family, Fiona and Harli, for your love and support.

To my mum and dad, Christine and Tom, for being an inspiration and instilling in me a hard work ethic.

To Andrew Mackenzie for your guidance; to Greg Jewson for keeping me grounded; to Karen Pini for giving me a start and being my other mum; to Dan Mckinnon for showing me what five star looks like.

To Bernadette Schwerdt, who has helped me to capture, then shape, all my crazy ideas into something for you to use and refer to while you build your business.

To the amazing team at Wiley who have taken this dream and made it a reality.

And to you, for trusting me to guide you with these words on your journey to success.

# INTRODUCTION

I will never forget Friday, 10 March 1989. I had just got home from school and was about to go kayaking. Mum was in the kitchen cooking dinner. My brother was in the garage fixing his bike. My sister was in the lounge watching *Happy Days*, which was an ironic viewing choice, considering what was about to happen.

I heard footsteps crunch on our gravel driveway. It wasn't Dad. He would never be home this early. It probably wasn't a visitor either. We didn't get many of those. We lived at the bottom of a long, steep, unsealed road nestled deep inside the darkened forest of the Ku-ring-gai Chase National Park, around 30 kilometres north of Sydney. The little street we lived on was so narrow you had to do a seven-point turn just to reverse direction.

The visitors we did get were often architectural boffins from a New York design magazine or a judge from the Royal Institute of Architects having a sticky-beak at our house. Dad spent seven years designing and building it. He was one of Australia's foremost architects and specialised in creating complicated structures made from concrete, steel and glass for the rich and famous. Take a look at any of the riverfront mansions dotted along the foreshore of the Hawkesbury River—the ones with multiple levels, unusual roof lines or those perched precariously on the side of a sandstone cliff—and odds are my dad designed it.

# Who knew Australia had sheriffs?

Our riverfront home was extraordinary. It spanned 11 levels, had five bedrooms, a boatshed, a pool, a pontoon, a wharf, a turret and a flagpole. From the outside it looked like a cylinder on top of a cube, on top of an oblong. Yes, it was that kind of house and he was that kind of architect. Mum and Dad were hugely social, had a wide network of friends and loved to entertain, so we spent most weekends having BBQs on our boat, swimming in the river or swanning around the yacht club.

The crunching of footsteps on the gravel grew louder. I looked out the window and saw two men walking down our driveway. One wore a dark-brown suit the colour of soil. The other wore a crisp, white shirt and black trousers with a large gold badge pinned above his shirt pocket. Strapped around his hips was a tool bag, similar to a builder's belt. It held an array of implements including a walkie-talkie, a bundle of keys and most ominously, a gun.

There was a knock at the door. I raced out, fearful that Mum would get there first. I was only 15, but I felt responsible for her—for the whole family really (the perils of being a first-born boy). Whoever it was or whatever these people wanted, I would be the first line of defence.

Mum beat me to it. She opened the door and was greeted with the six words that would change our lives.

'Mrs Simmat? This house is repossessed.'

The man with the shiny gold badge took out a hammer from his builder's belt, fished a nail from his top pocket, and with one heavy punch, pinned a two-page letter to our front door.

He then read out the note with android efficiency:

'By the order of the State Bank of NSW, I hereby advise you that due to financial default on the mortgage held by said bank, I, as the sheriff of the State of NSW, instruct you to vacate this house within 72 hours.'

The man in the brown suit, the bank manager, with whom my parents had been friends, stood a few steps behind the sheriff, unsmiling. He studiously avoided my mother's glare, turned on his heel and crunched back up the driveway to the car waiting at the top of the hill.

Mum and I stared at each other. Surely this was a joke, or at worst, a case of mistaken identity. Us? Lose this house? This could not be happening. Where was Dad? At work, of course. Like many momentous events in our family life, it was my mother who was left to pick up the pieces.

But this was not a mistake. This was real. Very real.

Within 72 hours, we had packed up our entire five-bedroom house; the house my dad had built from scratch with his bare hands; that we had grown up in, loved and treasured; the house that had won prestigious architectural awards and graced a dozen magazine covers; the house that formed the foundation of my life—our lives— and connected us to this wonderful river and forest.

Three days later, we were out on the pavement in front of the house, surrounded by our suitcases, waiting for the removalist truck. Our neighbours, many of whom lived in houses designed by my dad, stood at the top of our driveway, looking down on this forlorn scene.

I will never forget the look in their eyes. Pity.

I will never forget the look in my dad's eyes. Shame.

My dear, hardworking dad. My proud, upstanding mum. Both reduced to this. And us three kids, kicking the dirt, wondering what the future held for us and what this 'new normal' would look like.

## What went wrong?

As a businessman, my father was a great architect. The troubles began when he partnered with a construction company. On paper it sounded great. He would design the dwellings; they would build them. But it was the 1980s, an era of excess, of *Dallas* and *Dynasty*, of dodgy deals, lax oversight and minimal regulation. Interest rates blew out from 7 per cent to 17 per cent. A business deal with a local council to redesign their entertainment complex went sour when the council reneged on the deal. An unethical bank manager decided he'd like to buy the house my dad built and wanted it at a bargain-basement price. It was a perfect storm.

In short, Dad's business went bust. The bank took our home and everything in it. We were left literally on the side of the street with nothing but our household effects and the clothes on our backs. Were it not for the generosity of our neighbours, we would have had to sleep where we were standing.

When the dust settled, we moved to a low-rent suburb on the wrong side of the tracks and took up residence in a little fibro shack. It was the kind of neighbourhood where burned-out cars took pride of place on the front lawn and broken windows never got repaired.

Dad tried to resurrect his business but the recession had hit hard so the demand for high-end architectural services evaporated. We went bankrupt—not in the legal sense but in every other way. Dad never really recovered from the humiliation of it all.

Am I scarred by what happened? Yes.

Am I bitter about what happened? Yes.

Am I motivated by what happened? You bet.

## My burning mission

That experience broke my dad, but it emboldened me. I saw with my 15-year-old eyes what happens when powerful institutions abuse their power; when influential people with dubious morals misuse their position for their own personal gain.

That experience created a burning hunger within me that continues to burn brightly to this day. That burn was to get back what

I had lost; to find a way to ensure that what happened to my dad never happened to me, or anyone else I cared about.

In that moment, standing on the side of the street, I vowed that I would:

- dedicate my life to finding the secrets of business success so that I could protect myself and others from falling prey to unscrupulous operators

- create an unbreakable business model that would survive a recession, a depression or any other kind of economic upheaval

- educate myself on every aspect of business—finance, sales, marketing, HR, technology—so that no-one could ever pull the wool over my eyes.

I didn't know how I was going to do it, but I did know I was going to do it.

## Is $20 million worth writing home about?

By Silicon Valley standards, my business success has been modest. I didn't build a $2 billion business, or even a $200 million business. But I did build a $20 million business in under 16 years from scratch. Sure, that's not a number that will have me ringing the opening bell on the New York Stock Exchange, but in most people's language, $20 million is a life-changing amount of money. It's certainly what could be crudely called, 'fuck-off money'.

So why should you read this book and take my advice? Why wouldn't you listen to people who have made far more money than me? People like Elon Musk or Warren Buffet or Jeff Bezos? Well, you can, and you should, but their life stories and business journeys probably won't help you build a business that others want to buy. Why? Because they are all extraordinary people, with exceptional talents and incredible timing; they are the outliers, the one-percenters, the unicorns. They were always going to succeed no matter who or what stood in their way.

We are not all like that. I'm certainly not. I am not being falsely modest when I say that I am not extraordinary or unique in any way, and I am not especially talented. I did not have exquisite timing, or intelligence, or a piece of must-have software. I didn't have money, contacts or a first-class education. I wasn't passionate about a particular topic or have a spectacular business idea. I didn't have a burning desire to change the world.

I just wanted to make as much money as I could so that I could get back what I had lost. And I did that. I built a business that became the country's leading accreditation, recruitment and business coaching consultancy. In 2022, after just 16 years in business I had a valuation of $20 million and was getting offers from buyers every few months. That business is now sold and I am now on track to build a $100 million global business-coaching empire.

Along the way, I discovered some insights that I wish I had known when I started out. If I knew then what I know now, I would have got to where I am going in half the time and with half the effort. I'd like to share those insights with you so that you don't have to make the same mistakes I made and you can protect yourself from making bad decisions that could cost you your livelihood.

## Who is this book for?

It's amazing how many business owners *start* a business without any concern for how they're going to *end* the business. I understand this completely. I was that person. I was the uber-technician; the 'expert'. I did everything wrong. I didn't delegate. I had no systems. I didn't track anything. I hired the wrong people, spent time on the wrong activities and was overly reactive to things that didn't matter.

I wrote this book for my 29-year-old self; the person I was when I started out and knew nothing about anything. I wrote it for those who want to do things the right way, the first time; for those who want to start with the end in mind. Read this book and discover the secrets of how to:

- build a business others want to buy
- create recurring streams of subscription-based revenue
- identify the top 15 drivers that make a business valuable
- know exactly what metrics buyers really look for when buying a business
- develop a repeatable, scalable sales pipeline that operates without your involvement
- win multimillion-dollar contracts from government and Tier 1 operators
- own 100 per cent of your business and fund it without external investors or partners
- spot the trends for what the 'next big thing' will be
- build a loyal team that works with minimal supervision yet delivers exponential results
- develop a world-class internship program that eliminates the need to hire expensive recruiters
- increase your social media following to attract lucrative partnerships and collaborations
- use best practice tools and techniques to hire and fire staff, coach underperforming executives and motivate your team
- sell anything to anyone at any time, ethically and elegantly.

Whether you're starting out or have been in business for decades, this book outlines the principles, policies, procedures, structures, systems, templates and checklists that will empower you to build a business others want to buy.

# Why trust me?

People say money can't buy happiness. That's bullshit. That's what people who don't have money say to feel better about not having money. Being poor is not fun. I've been there, done that and didn't like it. Money does not buy total happiness but it sure goes a long way to buying things that prevent sadness.

As I write this book, I am sitting here in my home in Narrabeen Beach, high up on the cliff, overlooking the ocean. My son is swimming in the pool, my wife is doing yoga on the deck and my dog is on my lap. I have a LandCruiser, five boats, a jet ski and a surf ski. I kayak every day, I rarely wear a suit, or shoes, and I do what I want, when I want. I recently won 'volunteer of the year' for my son's sailing school. I mentor practically anyone who asks me to do so, and spend most weekends with friends and family on my boat or at the yacht club. I have clawed back the life and lifestyle that was taken from me as a 15 year old and I am happy and content.

I don't say this to boast, or to big note. I say it because I've taken what was a very traumatic, life-changing event—watching my father lose everything he worked for—and used that horrendous experience to recreate my life.

I tell this story because I want to demonstrate that anything is possible.

I tell it because I want you to know that if you want to design a life, and enjoy it and not just endure it, then I have the formulas and the templates to help you re-invent, reinvigorate and reimagine what your life and business can be.

I have done it, and you can do it too. Just follow the recipe.

# How this high-school drop-out built a $20 million business

I was not a gifted scholar. In fact, I failed high school. I even struggled to get into TAFE, and that's saying something. After I left school, I completed a hospitality course, became a chef, laboured on building sites and then eventually clawed my way into a science degree, which turned out to be as useful as the 'g' in lasagne.

My career really began when I was 25 and landed my first job at Hornsby Council. Yes, it was as boring as it sounds, but it was life changing—not because it helped me figure out what I wanted to do with my life, but because it helped me figure out what I *didn't* want to do.

It taught me that I didn't want to work in a job where my wages and opportunity were capped; where I had to wear a suit every day; where I had no control over my time; where I had to ask permission to get time off to attend weddings, funerals and dental appointments. I knew I had to start my own business, but I had no idea what I should sell. I wasn't overly passionate about any topic, cause or sector.

As part of my council work, I'd done some auditing and assessment work and it was pretty easy, so when the opportunity came to do some auditing after hours and make some extra money, I grabbed it with both hands.

After four years of working for the council and doing random audit assessments after hours, I could see where the industry was headed. I knew the government was going to make accreditation an ongoing requirement for most industries, so in 2004, at the ripe old age of 29, I resigned from the council, struck out on my own as an accreditation specialist and launched Simmat and Associates.

It was a fancy name for what was effectively me and my dog in a one-bedroom apartment. But thanks to the inefficiencies of the Brown Cardigan men (more on them later) who weren't that keen on working very hard or creating any innovation, I was able to implement some new ideas that my clients appreciated and became successful pretty quickly. My core products were accreditation, audits, procedure manuals and systems for small- to medium-sized businesses and the occasional big corporate.

Within 10 years my business had grown to 14 people and turned over $2 million. It was modest growth but I had modest goals. We worked out of a three-bedroom weatherboard cottage in Frenchs Forest, 20 kilometres north of Sydney. It wasn't a fancy workspace. We had desks everywhere: in the kitchen, in the bedroom, in the hallway. It was, in every sense of the term, a cottage business.

## When love came calling

The business would have probably bumbled along and delivered me an ordinary income and average lifestyle had it not been for three significant turning points.

The first involved my girlfriend, Fiona. We had been dating for 10 years. I was desperately keen to marry her but she was content to let the relationship take its course. We had a mortgage together, so we were committed, but marriage eluded us. It came to a head in early 2008 when she resigned from her job as executive assistant to the CEO at Blackmores. She said, 'I'm heading to South America for three months. You can come if you want. If not, I'm going anyway.' I was desperate to join her, but I had this cumbersome business to manage and the thought of running it while hiking through the Amazon jungle seemed impossible. I'd been told by a few trusted sources that the internet reception in South America was patchy at best. How could I run the business remotely if I couldn't even send an email?

Fiona was all packed and ready to go. She lovingly taunted me with her plans. 'In February, I'll go to Mardi Gras in Rio. In April, I'll head down to the Amazon, and in May I'll do Lake Titicaca.'

Meanwhile I was knee deep in audits and procedures and racking my brain to see how I could create a system that would let me travel with her, while keeping tabs on the team back home.

I went with her to the travel agency and sat beside her as the agent took her through the itinerary. I should have felt happy for her but I felt sick. I was missing out on the trip of a lifetime, and potentially losing the love of my life.

As the dot matrix printer whirred in the background, Fiona said, 'Last chance. In or out?' I looked at her and realised that there was more to life than business, and that if I couldn't find a way to make this work then the business wasn't worth having. I said, 'I'm in! Let's do it!' Her eyes lit up. She hugged me, and said, 'About time!'

With the tickets booked, I now had to find a way to manage the business from the wilds of South America. I bought a hard-cover notebook and made a list of everything that needed to be done while I was gone. That list grew and grew and eventually became what's now known as The Book of 50, simply because it was a book that had 50 'to do' items in it.

I said to the team, 'I'll be gone for 12 weeks. While I'm gone, if you complete all of your prescribed tasks, and you have time on your hands, go to The Book of 50, pick a task and complete it. If you finish that, pick another one and do that. I don't want anyone twiddling their thumbs while I'm gone.'

When we arrived in South America, I discovered I could get better internet in Machu Picchu than I could in Mosman. I learned two important lessons that day: those 'trusted experts' who said I would never get internet coverage in South America were wrong, and in future I would challenge—or, as I call it, shit-test—all advice and assumptions.

This enabled me to call in once a week to check in on the team, provide some coaching and mentoring to those who needed it and then continue with my trek. The team functioned well, the work got done and everyone appeared happy. I was quietly pleased with the system I had put in place.

Fiona and I had a brilliant holiday. The ultimate was when she (finally) agreed to marry me on a moonlit night at the base of the Machu Picchu ruins. The trip was working out so much better than expected. After 12 weeks of extraordinary adventures, we returned home.

# What do you mean, 'we've got no clients'?

On my first day back in the office, I walked in and saw half the team in the tea room chatting, and the other half playing hallway cricket. From the scores on the whiteboard, it appeared they'd been having a multi-day tournament.

'Hey guys,' I said, 'Why aren't you working? Surely there's stuff to do in the Book of 50?'

They said, 'Yeah, but we did it all.'

'But what about the new clients coming through the pipeline. Surely that work needs to be completed?'

'There aren't any new clients coming through the pipeline,' they said.

'What do you mean there's no new clients?'

'You didn't put it in the Book of 50.'

'What? You mean I forgot to delegate sales?'

'Yep,' they said, making themselves a cup of tea and flicking through a magazine.

What a rookie error! I had been so focused on getting the current crop of client work done that I didn't think to set up a lead generation system that would bring in the next wave of clients. It seems ridiculous now to think that I would overlook such a critical function, but I did.

Like I said, I'm not extraordinarily talented or special in any way! I failed to adhere to the most basic rules of business:

*Keep the business coming in.*

*Fill the pipeline.*

*Be the rainmaker.*

There was other trouble brewing. I checked the bank balance and was completely shocked to discover that while there was enough money to cover payroll for the next month, there was next to nothing left after that. I was suffering on two fronts now. No sales and no cash flow.

This was the second turning point for me. I decided then and there that I would never take other people's word for how things were going, and I would never overlook anything, even something as basic as filling the sales pipeline. From that moment on, I made it my mission to create a bullet-proof lead generation system that would deliver a repeatable, scalable source of qualified leads. I would also build a dashboard containing 21 metrics that would enable me and any of my staff to see in an instant where we stood. With one click, we could track sales, leads, proposals sent, cash in, cash out, email open rates, click throughs, blog engagement, see who was hitting their KPIs, who wasn't, why not and what was needed to help them do so.

## Thank you, Kevin Rudd

The third turning point for the business was the global financial crisis (GFC) of 2008. It was a disaster for many, but a godsend for us. In addition to giving everyone $1000 to spend on a big-screen television, Kevin Rudd, the prime minister at the time, launched the Nation Building Economic Stimulus Plan, which funnelled billions of dollars into the building industry. This money was used to construct school halls, install pink batts, dig new roads and more. It had the desired effect. The building industry roared back to life. But there was a catch: to tender for any of these contracts, the supplier needed to be accredited. And guess who had the keys to the accreditation kingdom? We did.

We were perfectly positioned to take advantage of the upswell in demand. For a start, we had no work, so we had the capacity to take on new clients. Second, we had a well-trained team, a great track record and solid credentials to win the work. And third, the building companies were in such a hurry to get their accreditation paperwork sorted out, they accepted whatever price tag we put on the work.

We became the 'go-to' accreditation agency for any company who wanted to tender for government or Tier 1 work. We were swamped and our business grew like crazy.

## What even is accreditation?

For those unfamiliar with the world of international standards (and that would be most of us), there is a global governing body called the ISO (International Organisation for Standardisation). (You won't be the first to note that the ISO acronym is out of whack. In Greek, ISO means equal.) It is an independent body of expert assessors from a range of industries and they represent almost every sector and industry.

These assessors have universally agreed that if a company wants to own the mantle of being the 'best' at something, and be trusted to deliver the best service, safety, security or standard, then they need to pass a series of tests. Once passed, that company receives 'certification', which rubber stamps them to tender for multimillion- and multibillion-dollar contracts from governments and blue-chip corporates. From food safety, to occupational health, to cyber safety, to quality assurance, to customer service, if a company wants to tender for a contract, they need to attain accreditation in that sector to demonstrate they have met a certain standard.

As a trusted accreditation specialist, I had a seat at the table of Australia's most successful companies where their top executives shared with me in detail not only the secrets of their success, but more importantly, the secrets of their *failures*. It's well known that any system is only as strong as its single point of failure: that unique part of a business practice, supply chain or industrial system that, if it fails, stops the entire system from working.

I discovered very quickly that if you can work out how a company fails, you can work out how they will succeed. For a man eager to build a bullet-proof business model that could survive any economic headwinds, this education and experience was gold.

My team and I became so good at identifying what best practice looked like, in 2009 we rebranded Simmat and Associates to become Best Practice.biz to reflect our unique knowledge and expertise in enabling businesses to tender for these massive contracts.

How did we know what best practice was? We synthesised the thousands of manuals, procedures, handbooks, guidebooks, templates, scripts, policies, systems and structures from the hundreds of companies we worked with, and turned that knowledge into a five-step process that anyone could use to create best practice in their industry.

The formula we created forms the foundation of this book. In your hands, you hold the keys for how you can create 'best practice' in your industry and build a profitable business that will withstand the harsh glare of the steeliest corporate raider, institutional investor or mergers and acquisitions lawyer.

If you're ready to stand on the shoulders of those who have gone before you so that you can see into the distance and build a business others want to buy, let me be your guide. I've been there, done that and have the scars to prove it.

If I did it, anyone can.

# PART I

# MINDSET

I f you want to be successful, you need to know what success means to you. My advice? Start with the end in mind. For example, do you want to buy a fancy boat, live in a waterfront mansion and fly first class for the rest of your life? If so, you'll need to build a business possibly worth millions. You'll need to dedicate a large swathe of time to making it happen and be prepared to withstand the pressure and blowback that comes with building a substantial enterprise.

Maybe you want a simpler version of success, a lifestyle that lets you do what you want, when you want, how you want. You may not get to fly first class or drink fancy champagne, but you'll have the time and space to focus on the things that matter to you. As such, you may not need to work so hard or long to achieve this.

You can have what you want. But just get clear about what you want before you begin. This decision is important as it will dictate the type of business you need to build to generate the lifestyle you desire. Think big from the get-go. For a start, it gives you something to get excited about, and if you achieve a fraction of what you set out to achieve, you'll already be ahead.

Get these early decisions right and you'll create the foundations you need to turn a small idea into a big success.

# What does the 5-star experience look like?

# Chapter 1
# Why every 15-year-old boy needs a Karen Pini in his life

A ny teenage boy who grew up in the '80s will remember Karen Pini. Karen was a Miss World finalist, a *Playboy* model, an actress and the Lotto lady on Channel Nine. She was also my neighbour (I know—some kids have all the luck). She wasn't just my neighbour, though. She was my friend and became one of the most influential figures in my life.

Karen ran the Cottage Point Kiosk, a general store for the local community living in and around the Ku-ring-gai Chase National Park, 30 kilometres north of Sydney. The kiosk overlooked the Hawkesbury River and was the fulcrum around which the local boating community congregated. You could say the kiosk was a 'mixed business'. It was a convenience store, a coffee shop and a wharf; it offered boat hire, boat repairs, boat cleaning and much more. During the day it was a one-stop shop for sailors and their crews, and at night it came alive with music, food and lots of partying.

# My big break

When I was 15, just prior to Dad losing the house, Karen offered me a part-time job helping out behind the counter and serving customers. It was a good arrangement for both of us. The kiosk was located just up the street from where I lived, so I could walk to work after school each day and Karen could call on me at short notice if she needed help.

The job suited me on a range of levels. Mum was busy looking after my younger brother and sister. Dad was always working, his business was faltering and money was tight. To make matters worse, Mum was drinking a fair bit ('I'm an alcoholic because your dad's a workaholic!', she'd say). So, all in all, the atmosphere at home was pretty tense.

School was not going so well either. I was floundering and couldn't do a thing right. The kids hated me, and I hated them. The teachers at school thought I was a smart arse. They resented me for questioning anything and could see that I was more mature than the other kids, and unwilling to tolerate their inane utterings and idiotic policies.

It didn't help that my grades were poor too, which gave the teachers more ammunition to attack me. It wasn't that I lacked mental aptitude. I just didn't get what school was for. Why did I need to learn about the Magna Carta? Who cares about the Milford Sound? What's that got to do with life? School was a game, I didn't know the rules and I was losing big time.

## A new opportunity

Karen was at an interesting point in her life. She'd had a high-flying, high-profile career as a model and actress; she'd married a wealthy, well-known property developer and had three children with him. By any standard, you'd say it was a successful life. But as I got to know Karen, I discovered that the public image did not gel with the private reality.

The truth was her career as an actress and model was flailing and her finances were in disarray. She'd been ripped off badly by a manager and had not been paid for a large chunk of her work (including the *Playboy* centrefold). Her realtor husband was busy selling real estate in the city, so she was left to bring up three children and run a labour-intensive business that generated a lot of work for little return.

When Karen offered me a job, I said 'yes' instantly. It was a good fit for her and it was a great fit for me. I worked after school and on weekends and loved every second of it. It was fun, exciting and filled with interesting characters. From the kiosk window, I could see when a boat would arrive. I'd slide down the hand-rail in my board shorts and greet the guests at the wharf. I'd help them dock their boat, walk them up to the kiosk, sit them down, take their order and pour them a coffee.

While they enjoyed their meal, I'd clean their boat and stock it up with whatever they needed. When they departed, I'd give them tips on where to find the best fishing spots, the top swimming holes and the finest hiking trails. I was a veritable font of touristic knowledge!

At night, the kiosk turned into a fun palace. Yachties and their crews would hang out in the bar, play music, dance, eat, swim and party on until the sun came up. It was a fantastic way to spend the weekend—and I got paid to be there! For a hyperactive 15-year-old kid whose mum and dad weren't getting on that well at home, this was heaven.

As time went on and Karen could see that I was responsive, reliable and eager to learn, she gave me more responsibility. I hired staff, took care of the roster, ordered the food, designed the menu, balanced the books and managed the business. Karen increasingly turned to me for advice. I didn't know much about running a business but I gave her my honest opinion about what I thought, and to my amazement, she took much of what I said on board, and it worked.

Karen's belief in me helped me build my confidence at a time when I needed it most. Despite all the crap that was going on at home and school, I discovered that I had a positive energy; that I could anticipate people's needs and make them smile. I thought everyone had this ability but Karen helped me realise it was a unique trait, and a valuable asset. I am a naturally gregarious person, and I love being of service so this didn't even feel like work to me.

The business grew and I grew with it. Karen valued my involvement because she could take a much-needed breather from the physical rigours of running the business. I loved it because I got to hang out with adults who didn't treat me like an annoying kid. By the time I turned 16, I was the general manager of the store. People looked up to me. I was the manager, hiring and firing and managing the money. I was the boss! The power was intoxicating.

## The big fail

Blending my two worlds of school and work was challenging. It was like I was living parallel lives.

By day, I was being bullied and beaten up by square-headed boys who didn't know their arse from their elbow.

By night, I was at the kiosk, managing a team of people, mingling with multimillionaires, handling tens of thousands of dollars and being treated with respect by people I admired.

This split life I was leading was confusing. It made me distrust the education system. If school was meant to be preparing me for life outside of school, why was life outside school easier than being at school?

School did not end well. I failed dismally. I got one of the lowest marks of the year level. It was humiliating. I desperately wanted to enrol in a degree in construction management but I just didn't get the marks I needed. I was pretty depressed about it and felt like a failure.

Mum and Dad were not happy with my school results either. They were tertiary educated, valued intellectual endeavour and did not want to see me 'waste' my life working as a waiter at the kiosk.

## An offer too good to refuse

This failure forced me to recalibrate my goals and ask the question, 'What am I going to do with my life?' Mum was pretty smart about getting me motivated to do further study. She said, 'If you don't do further study, you have to pay rent. If you do further study, you don't have to pay rent.' This was an offer too good to refuse so I scoured the university guide to see what course would accept a high-school dropout. Nice move, Mum.

Meanwhile, Karen had introduced me to a man called Dan McKinnon. Dan owned the Cottage Point Inn, a five-star 'destination restaurant' for some of Sydney's wealthiest people. He gave me a job and trained me in the art of fine dining. This was a step up from the kiosk and I loved it. He taught me what it was to serve, put your ego aside, smile when you don't feel like it, drum up energy when you're tired, solve problems, make people feel good, ask incisive questions, think on your feet and deal with a wide range of people.

I loved the experience of working in this five-star dining restaurant so much, I enrolled in a two-year business diploma in hospitality at

Ryde TAFE. The course was a consolation prize really, but it served a number of purposes. It got Mum off my back, it got me free rent at home and it was the bridging course I needed to get into a proper university course.

I loved that course, and I was good at it. I did not skive off one class. I did not have one complaint from a teacher, tutor or patron. I went from flunking out in school to flying high at hospitality. It also taught me one of the most valuable lessons I have ever learned: how to turn every experience into a five-star encounter, even when the budget does not allow you to provide a five-star experience. It taught me how to imagine what a five-star version of something might look like and then work hard to offer that. Nowadays, no matter who I'm working with, or what I'm working on, the question I'm always asking is, 'What does the five-star version of this situation look like?' It has helped me find innovative solutions to seemingly intractable problems.

I learned more in my two years at the TAFE hospitality course than I did in 13 years of school. It was a formative experience. The course taught me how to be humble, to put my ego aside, deal elegantly with conflict, get to 'yes' and close the sale. It also taught me how to cook too: an essential life skill for all teenage boys! I think hospitality should be a compulsory high-school subject.

After completing this course and getting high distinctions all round, I was finally able to get into university. I enrolled in a Bachelor of Applied Science, which was also life changing, albeit in a different way. It taught me how to be a critical thinker, create systems and be methodical: all perfect qualities for my future business.

Looking back, I can see that the core principles I hold dear today—curiosity, empathy, friendliness—were instilled in me as a 15-year-old boy when I was trained, mentored and guided by some of the smartest, kindest people in the hospitality industry. These were guiding values that set me up for my next adventure and have served me well to this day.

If you fell ill and couldn't work, how long could your business survive?

# Chapter 2
# Why most small businesses fail

I f you fell ill and couldn't work, how long could your business survive?

A month? A year? A decade?

For most business owners, the sad reality is their company would shrivel up and die within the week.

Why? Because they *are* the business. Without them, nothing happens. If they stop, so does the business. They are what's known as 'technicians'. The term is not a pejorative, but it's not a compliment either, especially if you want to build a business others want to buy.

A technician is the person who *does* the work. They are a visionary architect, a brilliant baker or a talented coach. They often have a large and loyal fanbase, win awards, get great feedback and have clients clamouring to work with them. And that's the problem: the clients clamour to work with *them*.

If you were to tell me you're in the Top 100 of your industry, I would say 'Congratulations!', but I would also say 'I'm so sorry' because that is not a position you want to occupy. Being good at what you do is part of the problem because your identity and ego are caught up in *delivering* the service when you should be focused on *building* the business.

If you want to build a business others want to buy, you need to move from being a 'technician' to becoming an 'owner' as quickly as you can. The strategy for moving into the 'owner zone' will challenge, confront and confound you. It will take considerable skill and application, but if you want to build a business others want to buy, you need to be much more than a technician and dramatically change the way you currently operate.

## Why don't technicians build big businesses?

Michael Gerber popularised the 'technician' concept in his 1995 book, *The E-Myth*. This book influenced a generation of entrepreneurs. It certainly influenced me.

The 'E' refers to the word 'entrepreneur' and the title refers to the erroneous belief that an 'entrepreneur' is naturally gifted and equally good at doing the technical *and* the operational work of running a business.

The goal, as Gerber puts it, is to move through the three stages of being an entrepreneur and get to the 'owner zone' as quickly as you can. He identified the three stages of being an entrepreneur as:

1. technician
2. manager
3. owner.

Gerber posited the premise that if a technician doesn't or can't move into the owner zone, they will never get to build a sellable asset. Here's what each label means.

## The technician

A technician is somebody who does the bulk of the work that brings in the revenue. They:

- make and sell the product or service
- design the systems and processes
- write the sales copy
- send the invoices and do the administration.

## The manager

The manager 'manages' the people who do the work. They:

- turn the entrepreneur's vision into action
- directly manage tasks, projects or people
- keep the team accountable to the KPIs
- build the team, create the systems and provide structure and support.

## The owner

The owner is the dreamer, the visionary, the 'big picture' thinker. They:

- create a compelling vision and motivate the team to bring it to life
- think of new ways to do things
- build partnerships and collaborations
- create assets to be exploited for profit.

A business owner often gets stuck in the technician zone, which can have a deeply negative impact on the business, but because the technician gets so rewarded for being good at what they do, they find it very difficult to break out of this zone. As such, they can spend up to 95 per cent of their time in this zone and 5 per cent in the owner zone, when in fact the ratio should be reversed: they should be spending 5 per cent in the technician zone and 95 per cent in the owner zone.

Ultimately, going from technician to owner is a journey of building the people and the processes inherent in your organisation. A technician's first task is to find a manager to help them move out of the 'doing' zone and into the 'planning' zone. Without that manager, the entrepreneur has no hope of building a business that others want to buy.

# THE TOP SIX LIMITING BELIEFS THAT STOP TECHNICIANS FROM BUILDING SUCCESSFUL BUSINESSES

When I started Simmat and Associates, I was the quintessential technician. I did everything. It took me a few years to cotton on to what being an owner meant, but once I did, I pursued that goal with gusto. If you are still a technician three years after starting your business, you're wallowing around on activities that will not get you the result you want. You need to move out of this zone *now*.

Here are my top 6 limiting beliefs that stop you from doing so.

## Limiting belief #1

*If I stop doing the work, I will lose control and I won't know what my team is doing.*

It's scary not knowing what everyone is doing, but that's part and parcel of being an owner, and that's exactly what you *want* to happen.

You *need* to let go of the day-to-day minutiae and let your team focus on the execution of the plan.

You *need* to remove yourself so far from the daily operations that you couldn't manage it, even if you wanted to.

You *need* to set up the systems so that anyone can come into the team, read the manual, watch the video and do the task.

Your goal is to hire the right people, put the right systems in place and let the people run the systems. After all, what is a big business? It's just a small business with systems.

## Limiting belief #2

*I want to hire a team but I'm afraid they won't do as good a job as me.*

This is classic technician talk:

◆   No-one is as good as me

◆   No-one can do the job like me

◆   No-one knows the client like I do

◆   Without me, the work won't get done.

There's a lot of ego embedded in these beliefs. Unless you're George Clooney or Lady Gaga (and even then), most people are replaceable. Never forget: the cemetery is filled with irreplaceable people. Don't fall into the trap of believing that no-one can do what you do. Have you ever noticed that when you lose an 'irreplaceable' person, their replacement is often better?

But even if they're not, if you hire well and train your team correctly there's no reason why they can't deliver to at least 80 per cent of your high standard. You will still be ahead of the game because you will have built a system that tells everyone what the acceptable standard is. This gives you the time and distance to help you spot errors and variations in quality before the work leaves the office.

## Limiting belief #3

*I love doing the technician work. It's why I started the business in the first place. I don't want to stop doing that.*

You don't have to give up the technician work. If you follow the guidelines in this book, you can do more of it, on your terms, and get paid more for it. Your technical creativity can be codified. Think Andy Warhol and The Factory. He trained dozens of acolytes to create art in his distinctive style and sold each 'Warhol' artwork for millions of dollars.

Large-scale advertising agencies are adept at doing the same. They commodify their creativity by automating their briefing systems, which enables junior creatives to do the low-level grunt work while the 'superstar' creatives get the final edit (and credit) for what gets produced and put into the public domain.

## Limiting belief #4

*I don't like attending meetings. I like to be free and work to my own schedule.*

I get it. You're creative, you march to the beat of your own drum, you're a free spirit; and to be told that you have to attend regular meetings with your team and clients, at times that may not suit you, makes you feel constrained and claustrophobic.

As a technician working solo, you get to call the shots as to when and how often you turn up, but you need to show up *a lot* just to make things tick. If that's what you want, then by all means, continue to pursue the false belief that being a technician gives you freedom. It gives you freedom to turn up when you want, but it doesn't give you the freedom to *not turn up at all*.

Conversely, a business owner committed to turning up on a regular basis for *a set period of time*, maybe five to seven years, will eventually never need to turn up *at all*—because they've sold the business for millions of dollars. They're out on their boat, sipping Margaritas and swimming in the Maldives.

Meanwhile, you as the technician, the person who loves their 'freedom', still needs to turn up, again and again, *forever*. If that's your definition of 'freedom', by all means, continue to operate as a technician.

## Limiting belief #5

*I need to know how everything is done in case something breaks down and it needs to be fixed.*

If you're the sort of person who says, 'Get out of my way, I'll fix this!' then you need to move towards being the person who *can't* fix it.

One billionaire business owner I know (who built his business from scratch) deliberately didn't learn how to update his website so that if he was ever called upon to do it, he couldn't, even if he wanted to. He knew it was a low-value task and that his time was better spent elsewhere.

Make it your mission to coach others to become an extension of you, and teach them how to be a team of world-class technicians so that you can focus on bigger, higher value tasks that make a difference.

## Limiting belief #6

*I don't identify as a leader. I don't want to be the 'boss' of other people.*

The hard truth is it can be lonely at the top. It can feel isolating. These feelings come with the territory. That's why CEOs have their own clubs and networks. It's a unique position that brings with it a unique set of rewards and risks. Being an owner is not a popularity contest. You will make tough decisions that others don't like. Don't try to be best mates with your team. You pay their wages and that creates a power imbalance. If you're lucky, some of your team may turn out to be good and loyal lifetime friends, but while they work for you, you will always be the boss and as such, you will never truly be 'one of the gang'.

If you spend all your resources of time, skill and money in the technician zone, you'll have a nice life, be good at what you do and win some awards, but you won't build a sellable asset.

If you want to build a business others want to buy, you need to change your mindset and start acting less like a technician and more like an owner.

# We are all going to die one day. Act like it.

Anonymous

# Chapter 3

# Do you get it, want it and have capacity?

B y my calculations, right now, as I write, I have around 40 years left to live, which is 14 240 days. That sounds rather dramatic, but I think we all need to be a bit more cognisant of how little time we have left to live.

It's all relative, of course.

Ask a teenager what they want from life and they'll say, 'I want to sleep in.'

Ask an octogenarian what they want from life and they'll say, 'I want to wake up!'

I have so little time left (no, I'm not terminally ill, I just love life and want to get the most out of those 14 240 days) that I feel compelled to help my staff get the most out of *their* days too. Work plays such a major role in most people's lives that it's fair to assume that if they don't like work, they probably don't like life very much either. If they're unhappy, they're more likely to leave their job, and I don't want that for them, or for me. Hiring is expensive. I want my staff to stay for as long as possible.

## The mother load

When a journalist asked comedian Hannah Gadsby how she 'identifies', she said, 'I identify as *tired*'.

She's not alone. Most business owners of a certain age are. Many of those I work with are running ragged. They're up at 5 am, at the gym by 6 am and at work by 7 am. They work full tilt for 10 hours, skip lunch, get home, have dinner with the wife and kids, crack open a bottle of wine, blast through a bunch of emails and hit the pillow at 11 pm. They get up the next day and do it all over again. Living the dream? I don't think so.

Working women with children have it even harder. They're like Ginger Rogers: they do everything the man does, but in high heels and backwards. Not only do they put in the same hours as their partner, they're often responsible for child care, cleaning, food preparation, homework supervision, housework and more. Finding time for the gym or a catch-up with the girls? That'll have to wait.

One woman I know, after mopping her kitchen floor, puts the chairs upended on the table and leaves them there until her husband gets home, to make visible to him the invisible work she does to keep the home and hearth ticking over. I'm stereotyping the gender distribution of labour here, but for the most part, this is how the division of chores pans out in most heterosexual households.

When I ask my clients if they're enjoying life, many of them, especially the women, say, 'Not much. I trust it will get better.' I wouldn't bet on it. It's safe to say that if nothing changes, nothing changes.

So, for those working crazy hours with no respite, unless they face the reality of their predicament, and take active steps to change it, their lives will continue to be stressful and unpleasant. That's not good for employees, and it's not good for employers, either. Unhappy staff are unproductive staff; unhappy staff tend to leave, and can cause all sorts of problems on the way out.

So, what role can you, as a business owner, play in helping your staff get more out of life? What can you do to ensure your staff have a sustainable work–life balance? Is it your business what life looks like for a team member after they leave your workplace and head home? I think it is.

## How to hire the right people

I work hard to help my staff find a satisfying work–life balance. I don't just pay lip service to the concept. I cannot see the point of working your staff so hard they have no time to have a home life. So, I take steps to help create an environment that suits my staff so they can have the best of both worlds.

There's a level of self-interest here. That self-interest starts with choosing the right staff to work for me. Hiring is always a hit-and-miss affair, but over the years I've gotten better at it. I now ask candidates three questions that help me filter out who is most suitable for the task at hand, who will get the job done and who is most likely to stick around. These questions have proven remarkably efficient in helping me hire A-grade players, spot B-grade players who can be coached to become A-grade players, and actively avoid C-grade players.

I ask these questions because I've been burned in the past by people who say one thing, and do another. They tell me how good they are, how much they want the job, how hard they'll work. They get the role but their hype doesn't live up to their reality; they're not half as good as they say and they can't do the job at hand. That's a costly own goal. I need to prevent that from happening.

These three questions help elicit emotional reactions that are imperceptible to the untrained eye. But if you are good at reading people and noticing the non-verbals, as I am, you get a better picture of how truthful their answers really are. (I have my mother to thank for that. More on that later.) I can see when a question makes a candidate flush, blush or blink. I am on the lookout for these signs because when their words are incompatible with their body language, I know something is up.

## The three key questions

Hiring well starts with asking these three key questions at the early stage of the interview process. Each question leads to more questions and each will uncover the truth about how appropriate this candidate will be for the job at hand, how badly they want this job and how good they'll be at it.

1. Do you *get* it?

    • Do you understand the job on offer?

    • Do you understand the KPI metric you are being asked to reach?

    • Does that metric or number motivate you?

    • Have you read the job description in detail?

    • Do you understand what every task and obligation means?

    • Do you fully understand the role this job plays in the wider functioning of this company?

    • Do you have the skills and experience to deliver on the job at hand?

    Assuming they say 'yes' to those questions, I then ask:

2. Do you *want* it?

    • Now that you know exactly what the role entails, do you honestly, genuinely, with no reservations want *this* job?

- Is there another job that you had your eye on (but didn't get), making this role the booby prize?

- Are you interested in this role because you've got your eye on the prize of a bigger job a few rungs above this one?

- Do you see yourself staying in this same role for at least three years?

Assuming they know what the job entails—they 'get' it—and they wholeheartedly desire the job at hand—they 'want' it—my final and perhaps most important question is…

3. Do you have the *capacity* to fit this job into your life?

- Do you have the time, mental preparedness, skills, experience, desire and space to fully commit to this role?

- Is there anything going on in your life that will prevent you from completing this job to the standards I have outlined in the earlier questions?

- Is there anything that could prevent you from completing this job in the allocated time?

## Why do I ask these three questions?

We hire for will and train for skill so we take a lot of time in our hiring process to ensure we get the right people, in the right job, for the right reason.

Hiring is easy. Firing is hard. (Or as we say in the recruitment business, 'hiring is guessing, firing is knowing'.) It's costly, draining on everyone and leaves a bad taste in the mouth for all concerned. It's much harder to get someone out of an organisation than it is to get them in, so we spend a lot of time ensuring we get the right people in so that we don't have to worry about moving them out.

## Why do I ask if they 'get' this job?

Can we assume the candidate has fully read the position description, understands the KPIs and knows exactly what they're getting into? No, we can't assume that. People often apply for jobs they're not qualified for, land the job and then spend half a year working out how to do it, on my dime. That's not on. They clearly don't 'get it'. It's my job to decipher what their motivation for taking the role is, *before* they take the role. That's why these three questions are so important.

## Why do I ask if they 'want' this job?

Surely that's self-evident? Why would they apply if they didn't want it? You may notice, I specifically ask, 'Do you want *this* job?' I don't want someone coming in who has their eye on another job within the organisation. You might be thinking, 'Don't I want someone who wants to climb the ladder? Shouldn't I hire a person with ambition and a drive to succeed?'

Well, yes and no. Don't get me wrong. I am not anti-ambition. I truly want people who are eager to progress. However, when I engage a new team member, I need them to want to be in the role for which they're being hired for at least three years. If they're ambitious, and you're not evaluating and updating their role within that time frame, they are likely to leave. By the time they're competent and firing on all cylinders, they already have one foot out the door and will start to neglect their current responsibilities. A leader needs to be cognisant of this so that they can get the most out of their worker but also keep them motivated enough to stay on and grow and evolve into a new role. That's why I ask this question.

## Why do I ask if they have the 'capacity'?

The last question, 'Do you have the capacity to fit this job into your life?' is often the clincher that cuts people out of the race. 'But,' you ask, 'Isn't that up to them to work out? Is that any of my business?' It is my business. If they can't physically dedicate the time to the job at hand due to outside pressures, then I need to know that.

## Fair exchange

Few people take on a job with me because they think, 'You know what? This guy has a great business. I'd love to help him make more money so he can work less, drink nice wine, fly first class and spend more time on his boat.'

That's not how people work, is it? People are self-interested and take jobs for the wrong reasons all the time. They take a job to secure a mortgage, pay off a debt, get work experience, placate their partner, make friends.

So, we both want something from each other but the reality is I am a for-profit business and I expect results for the money I pay my team. It's called fair exchange. I give you some money. In return you complete these tasks. If you don't complete these tasks, then you're taking my money for work not completed, and that's not fair exchange.

But let's say you ask those three questions, and the person answers them as honestly as they can, and you hire them. But when they arrive, it doesn't quite go to plan. They didn't fully understand the role in detail, they are now unable to be as committed as they once thought or maybe they just hid the truth because they really needed the money. This leads to another question.

## The four-word killer question

The killer question you need to ask to uncover the root cause of any kind of conflict is:

*What's on your mind?*

It's deceptively simple but incredibly powerful. Made famous by business coach Michael Bungay Stanier in his book, *The Coaching Habit*, I use this question all the time.

I follow it up with, 'And what else?'

Rinse and repeat until every objection, complaint or concern has been exhausted. Now you can start to find a solution.

It never fails to work.

Here's a case study where I didn't ask the right questions at the hiring stage, how I dealt with it (using the killer question) and how the situation could have been avoided in the first place.

## HOW TO KEEP YOUR TEAM HAPPY

In 2019, I hired Jessica, our customer service co-ordinator. She keeps the cash coming in. It's an important job. She's great with detail, meticulously organised and a hard worker. After a few months, I noticed she was looking tired; not the happy Jessica I'd seen when she started in the role. I had also noticed she was absent a lot and that her work was not getting done. In addition, she'd told her manager a few fibs about where she was and what she was doing when she was meant to be at work. I needed to find out what was going on.

In one of our regular catchups (and you must schedule regular—at least bi-weekly—catchups with your team) I asked her, 'How are you going?', and followed up, as always, with, *'What's on your mind?'*, my sideways question for getting to the bottom of an issue quickly.

She broke eye contact, her breathing quickened and a pink bloom appeared at the base of her throat. I could tell that what she was about to say was either going to be the full-blown truth, or a blatant attempt to cover up an issue that was truly troubling her.

It was the former.

She said, 'Kobi, I know you truly believe that everyone has the right to have a harmonious work–life balance, but for me it's just not possible. I don't think I can do this job any more. I can't work here and take your money when I'm not able to complete the job.'

My first impulse was to react: to encourage her to stay, to tell her it will be all right, that it will all work out. I didn't want to lose her. I had just hired her! (When confronted with moments of panic, the temptation is to rush to a solution, fix the problem and go straight to advice. Try not to.)

What's needed at times like this, however, is patience and curiosity; a genuine desire to get to the heart of why someone feels this way. It's about taking the time to go deeper and get to the root cause of an issue.

'Jessica, I can see something's troubling you. *What's on your mind?*'

She struggled to hold back the tears.

'I just can't cope,' she said. 'I have two children at home, both at primary school. I drop them off, I pick them up, make the meals, do the housework, help with homework and put them to bed. My husband works full time, he leaves before they get up, and he gets home after they've gone to bed so it's all on me. It's a lot.'

'That sounds like a heavy workload, Jessica,' I said. '*What else is on your mind?*'

She shifted awkwardly in her chair, unsure whether to add more fuel to the fire. I nodded gently to let her know I was open to hearing whatever she had to say.

'On top of that, I have elderly parents who need help and transport to medical appointments.'

'I imagine that would be very stressful,' I said. '*And what else is on your mind?*'

'I don't like being dishonest with you or the others, making excuses for why I'm late in or early to leave. I take work home to finish, but by the time 9 o'clock rolls around and the kids are in bed, I'm exhausted and I just fall asleep. Then the next day kicks in and I'm behind before I've started and that just creates more stress and anxiety.'

'That sounds exhausting. *And what else?*'

She was on a roll now.

'Okay, this is getting personal, but my health is suffering as well. I don't get to the gym, I don't eat well, I buy takeaway for dinner, which makes me feel like a terrible mother, and it's costly. My husband is kind of old school and he wants me to look slim and trim for him, and I want to look nice for him too, and myself, but the thought of going to the gym just exhausts me and besides, when would I have the time?'

*'And what else?'*

'I need this job, Kobi. I need the money. We have a big mortgage — we're in Sydney. Who doesn't? I need to support my parents too. I can't take a pay cut as that will just cause more pressure as we'll be short of money.'

*'Is there anything else?'* I asked. I figured I was getting to the crux of the problem now (and this closed question is a great way to bring a discussion to a head).

She shook her head. 'I think I've dumped just about every problem I have on you,' she said. 'Thank you for listening.'

Jessica's story did not surprise me. It is one of many I have heard over the years. Strong, competent, dedicated women pushed to the edge by the competing demands of work, finance, fitness and family. They suffer in silence, bust a gut to get things done and wind up exhausted, depleted and on many occasions, depressed. It's not a recipe for creating happy families or a happy workforce.

I could have jumped to conclusions. I could have jumped to a solution. But none of those strategies would be as powerful as actually finding out what was *on her mind*. I gave her the time and open space to tell me exactly what was going on for her. I fully understood her issue and could now come up with a solution. I didn't want to lose her. She was great at what she did. But she was right: the situation was untenable for all of us.

## WHAT *DON'T* YOU LIKE DOING?

To solve this issue and come up with a workable solution for us both, I needed to know what exactly Jessica's problem was. I could ask her, 'So Jessica, what do you want?' but in my experience, people don't know what they want. They do, however, know what they *don't* want.

Here's how I helped Jessica find a solution to her problem.

## HOW TO KEEP YOUR TEAM HAPPY (*CONT.*)

'Jessica, can I ask you a few questions about what you've just told me?'

'Sure,' she said, dabbing her eyes with a tissue.

'It seems like you're overwhelmed and exhausted.'

She nodded.

'If we could take away some of the responsibilities in this role, what would you like to get rid of that would make you happy, or happier? *What don't you like doing?*'

She thought about it and said, 'I don't like ringing people and talking to them. I find that stressful.'

I understood. English is her second language and being a softly spoken introvert, dealing with phone-based conversations would be stressful.

'Okay, so let's take that outbound phone work off your plate. What else don't you like doing?'

'I don't like the morning commute. It takes me over an hour to get to work. I don't like having to hide the fact I'm dropping my kids at school either.'

'Okay. We can stagger your hours so you can avoid peak hour and drop your kids at school. What else would need to happen to make you feel happier in the role?'

'I'd like to drop down to four days a week so that I can take care of the house and get a bit of time for myself on that one day off.'

'Jessica, let's move you to a four-day week.'

'That's great, but I can't afford to drop a day of work, Kobi.'

'You don't have to. I'll keep your salary as it is.'

She looked at me as if I was mad!

'You mean I can have everything I want, work less and still get paid the same?'

'Yes. That's what I mean.'

Her eyes welled up with tears. 'Thank you, Kobi. I won't let you down.'

'Jessica, we want you to stay here for as long as you want. We value you and want you to be happy. If your life is not panning out the way you planned and work is a big part of why that's happening, then it's not just your problem, it's mine too. I can ignore it at my peril and the result is you either stay and you're unhappy, which is bad for team morale, productivity and customer service. Or you leave and I have to replace you, hire someone new and retrain them to retain them. That's bad for the team, costly to the business and a massive waste of resources.'

The reality for Jessica was that she gets it and wants it but *she did not have the capacity to do the job.* She understood the job, she wanted it, but she didn't have the time in her life to commit fully and properly do the job for which she was hired.

Whose fault is that? Hers? A bit, for not being honest with me at the interview. It's mine too, for not asking the question and exploring it more fully at the interview. So, it's on both of us to fix it. Yes, I could move her on and find someone else and train them up and possibly have the same or other issues with the new person. But Jessica's really, really good at what she does and I didn't want to lose her.

Jessica got what she needed. A more flexible workplace, permission to put her family first when needed, less work—which was draining her—with no pay cut. And she didn't have to skulk around pretending she was working when she wasn't.

The result?

Jessica has been with us for several years now. She's still in the role for which she was originally engaged, she's more productive than ever because she's working to her strengths. We eliminated the things she doesn't want to do, which means she's got more energy to take on new tasks that fall within her sweet spot, which means we don't need to hire others to do that work. I don't expect staff to work weekends, but on the odd occasion when I've needed help to complete an important project, Jessica has been there for me, ready and willing to help. Swings and roundabouts.

You're probably thinking, 'Well, it's okay for you Kobi to give her everything she wants, cut her work load and pay her more. I can't afford to do that.'

Here's the thing. I couldn't afford not to. Yes, I took a hit with the four-day week on a five-day salary but it was worth it to keep her. The cost to hire, fire and retrain would be more than the extra day's salary so financially it was cheaper to give her an extra day off, build that loyalty and make her happy. The other concessions weren't expensive or difficult to accommodate. They just required some rescheduling and clear communication with other members of the team.

# How to help your team members exploit their true potential

According to Indeed.com, the average cost of a mis-hire is 200 per cent of an annual salary, so it pays to get hiring right. I don't leave it to chance. I put all my candidates through PXT Select. This online assessment tool uses scientifically validated data to measure cognitive ability, behavioural traits and interests as they relate to preferred traits for a given job. It helps me place the right people in the right roles.

In addition to that, I use these developmental questions to help my new hires discover what they really want in a role, and what they really don't want.

- What do you want to do more of?
- What are you interested in?
- What excites you in this role?
- What could we add to this role that would make you happy?
- Where do you see yourself in the business?

If they can't answer these questions, ask them the opposite:

- What do you want to do less of?
- What are you *not* interested in?
- What bores you or tires you out in this role?
- What could we get rid of in this role that would make you happy?
- Where do you *not* see yourself in the business?

If a team member is struggling, you can pretend it's not happening or you can face it head on. Find out what need is not being met and if you can help them fix it, they'll become loyal and long-standing team members for their working life.

# My Book of 50 is not just a 'to-do' list — it's a 'who-I-am' list.

# Chapter 4

# The Book of 50 (and how it changed my life)

T here are two types of people in this world: those who make lists and those who don't. I fall firmly into the former. I get it from my mother. She was so committed to list-making: if 'feed the kids lunch' was not on the list, we didn't get fed. Lists are brilliant for chunking down complex or unpleasant tasks into bite-sized activities that can be diarised and done with minimal indecision.

People criticise list-making as they say it creates stress and results in an endless parade of incomplete activities. But lists help me get things out of my head, prioritise goals and immerse myself in a task so completely that the outside world falls away. They help me enter what Mihaly Csikszentmihalyi famously called 'the flow'.

While I traipsed around South America, I used the Book of 50 to keep my team on track. Other than that little oversight of failing to add 'Get more sales' on the list, the system worked well. It served me so well while I was gone, I kept it going when I got back.

It's been in operation for more than 20 years now, and has become my 'go-to' system for productivity and goal-setting. My list has a lot more than 50 items on it (a *lot* more!) but the 'Book of 50' is what everyone calls it now.

## How did the Book of 50 get started?

The Book of 50 began as a series of post-it notes. I'd write a task on a post-it note, stick it to the bookshelf above my computer and when the task was completed, I'd take the note down. If the task didn't get done, the note didn't come down. It was a very effective system as it put my goals directly in my line of vision and kept me focused.

The only problem was, I'd have up to 30 A5 post-it notes dotted around the room. When I opened the window and the wind blew, the notes fluttered like delicate Tibetan prayer flags. It got so unwieldy I couldn't work out which goal to focus on, so I took all the post-it notes down, transcribed the tasks into a hard-cover notebook, and that became my Book of 50.

Whenever something comes into my mind that needs doing, or I think of a goal I want to achieve, it goes on the list. It could be a massive goal, like 'I want to sell my business for $20 million', or a tiny one like 'Ring the electrician to install some downlights in the rumpus room'.

I sit down with the book each evening before I go to bed, flick through it, identify the important activities that need to be done, put them on a separate list, and that becomes my action plan for the following day. This constant flicking between big goals, little goals, small tasks and major tasks helps keep me balanced and on track and provides a big-picture perspective.

## Keep the bubbles straight

When I was five, my dad taught me to sail. We started out in a little dinghy. 'Take the helm and set your destination,' he'd say, 'and if the bubbles in the wake are straight, you'll get to where you want to go.' The Book of 50 is my version of keeping the bubbles straight. It steers me towards my desired destination.

This is what my Book of 50 looks like.

You can see that I put a check box next to every activity. When the task gets done, I tick the box so I don't need to look at it again. If a task needs to be completed by someone else, I put their initials beside the task to remind me that it is with them, and then I make another note to follow up with them. It's a self-perpetuating loop that ensures everything gets captured and nothing gets lost. The only time I forget to do something is when the item does not get put on the list.

My 10-year-old son said, 'Dad, why don't you just use Notes on your iPhone?'

I said, 'It works better if I use pen and paper.'

He said, 'What's pen and paper?'

No, he didn't really say that, but the vilification of the humble pen and paper had to stop.

'Okay, smartie pants,' I said. 'If you don't want to use pen and paper, show me on the phone where you keep your list. Show me how you remind yourself. How are you going to tick your goals off? How are you going to give yourself gratitude in two years' time to look back over the things you've done?'

My millennial staff also chide me about being so analogue in a digital world. They say, 'Hey Kobi, there's an app for that.'

I tell them, 'I know. I've tried all of them and they don't work. If you can show me a digital version of my Book of 50 that is as accessible, visual and easy to use as this, I will use it.' They try, but they are yet to convince me.

I am not a luddite. On the contrary. I have always been an early tech adopter. I live and breathe my Google Calendar. I was a cloud-based business when most thought the data really did reside in the actual cloud. I spent the best part of $300 000 creating proprietary software that contained up to 20 dashboards. With one click I know how every aspect of my business is tracking. I built a staff intranet before most people knew what the internet was. I love tech, but when it comes to making lists, I love my analogue Book of 50 more.

People often ask how I make notes and keep track of mental thought bubbles when I'm out and about, in the car or travelling. It's simple. I make a note in the Notes app, or I use my Voice Memo or

Dragon Dictation to dictate it, and then I email or text it to myself. The Sticky Note app is also awesome. Somehow or other, I get the note to myself and then it all goes into the Book of 50.

## How to accomplish unpleasant tasks

Are there tasks on my list that I don't want to do? Absolutely. What business owner likes to revamp their website, negotiate their office lease or choose an IT provider? Yet those activities underpin a host of other important profit-generating activities that form the backbone of a successful business.

I constantly flip back and forth through the pages, looking for the stuff that's difficult to do, asking, 'What's the hardest thing I can do right now that's going to get me closer to my goal?' Doing the uncomfortable stuff is what really moves things forward.

Before I put anything on my list, I ask these five critical questions:

1. Why does this item need to be on the list?

2. What role does it play in helping me achieve my bigger, more exciting goal?

3. What benefit will I derive when this task is completed?

4. Is this task important or not important? Urgent or not urgent?

5. If it's not urgent and not important, why is it on the list in the first place?

The list helps me get motivated. I tell myself, 'When you've done this thing, you can go out on the boat, go out for lunch or go for a surf.' (Sometimes I add an item I've already done that wasn't on the list just so I can get the feel-good hit that comes with checking it off. ☺)

The Book of 50 also helps me subconsciously program myself to achieve my goals. For example, every time I read the list, my brain makes neural connections between what I have and what I want.

When I read a book, attend an event or meet with my team or clients, my reticular activating system is whirring away in the background, looking for ways to turn potentialities into actualities.

My bookshelf groans under the weight of more than 40 volumes of my Books of 50. Each contains the history of my personal and professional life. Every page is dated, so I can go back in time and see what I was thinking and doing on that day. I can tell you in granular detail how every goal I have ever achieved was attained. When I'm feeling low, or flat, or the imposter syndrome flares up, I flick back and it reminds me of who I am, why I am here and what I need to do next. It also reminds me of how far I have come, the challenges I have faced and the successes I have built.

My Book of 50 is not just a 'to-do' list — it's a 'who-I-am' list.

# Profit is the only thing that matters.

# Chapter 5

# Don't wear 'busy' as a badge of honour

B y 2014, my accreditation business had 14 staff, 100 clients and $2 million in revenue. Our core products at the time were writing operations manuals, conducting audits, and delivering occupational health and safety training. All the metrics I valued were ticking up, the clients were satisfied and my staff enjoyed the culture we had created. I was as busy as a one-armed brick layer, but I was happy. The business was going great guns.

To celebrate landing a new contract, I went out to a nice restaurant with my wife and three other couples. There was a bit of one-upmanship going on with the men in the group, each of whom owned a small business.

'We just took on a new hire,' said one. 'A fabulous guy. We poached him from an international investment bank. He's expensive, but worth it.'

'We just moved to a new office,' said another. 'Twice the size of what we had to accommodate all our new staff. We'll probably have to move again now we've won this monster contract.'

I'd had a few wines under my belt so when my turn came to spruik my achievements, I was well primed.

'I've just bought a new boat. A Halvorsen 40' Flybridge Cruiser. It's too big for what we need, but we'll get used to it. Ha ha.'

I was glad to get home that night. The constant one-upmanship was draining. I gave as good as I got but I was exhausted. On the other hand, I did feel quietly proud that I was able to match them dollar for dollar for what I had achieved, and then some. I had worked really hard and I was pleased with where I was at.

I went to work the next day. My CFO came into my office and sat down. She was on the brink of tears.

'Kobi, the ATO sent us a bill,' she said.

'Okay. For how much?'

'$100 000.'

My head spun.

'Whaaat? I thought it was going to be for around $30 000.'

'So did I, but they reassessed our tax obligations and readjusted the figure. We have seven days to pay it.'

'Well, pay it.'

'I can't.'

'Why not?'

'We don't have enough money in the account.'

'How much do we have?'

'Nothing.'

'What do you mean *nothing*?'

'We have enough for salaries, rent and the car leases, but once those obligations are paid, there's nothing left. We can't pay this tax bill. We'll be trading while insolvent if we do.'

I felt my father's shadow loom over me and I felt physically sick at the situation facing me. Could history repeat itself? Would I have my house taken off me just as my father had? It was entirely possible. The reality was we had sales, revenue, users, cash flow and all the other metrics that made us look successful, but we didn't have any *profit*.

I had been so dedicated to reinvesting in the business, training up the team, buying equipment, upgrading our offices and leasing vehicles, that I had overlooked setting aside some funds as profit. It sounds so ridiculous now, but in the heat of battle when I was trying to scale quickly, putting aside funds as profit just seemed pointless. Surely the money would be better used elsewhere where it could be working harder?

As it turns out, the answer is 'no'.

That boozy performative display of 'look how successful I am' at dinner the night before, coupled with the sobering reality of a tearful CFO worried sick we didn't have the funds to pay our tax bill, gave me pause for thought. If this was 'success', I needed to reassess my goals.

## A startling betrayal

This tax issue and lack of profitability were not the only issues I was facing.

Unbeknown to me, two of my 'trusted' staff members had set up a competitive company, while still working for me, and had been poaching my clients. Their modus operandi was to submit a quote from my company, and then minutes later, submit a cheaper quote for the same job under their company banner and win the tender. They took dozens of clients. No wonder we were struggling.

When I confronted them they denied it, but I found the paper trail that documented their subterfuge. They quit before I could sack them. I was happy to see them go, but the experience was heartbreaking. I had given these guys their first break, trained them up and taught them everything I knew. They were on six-figure salaries, far more than what I earned, and I had given them everything they had ever asked for. I couldn't believe the betrayal.

I needed to do things differently.

## Effort vs results

Up until then, being busy had been my badge of honour.

*Busy* meeting with prospects who didn't get it, didn't want it or didn't have the capacity to pay.

*Busy* presenting at industry events to people I didn't like or respect trying to bolster my brand and gain their imprimatur.

*Busy* with unimportant and non-urgent items that did not make a difference or move the dial in any way.

No more.

From now on, I would only focus on what made a difference to the bottom line. From now on, I would be ruthless in my pursuit of efficiency but most importantly, my pursuit of profitability.

I went through every expense, line by line, and deleted or cancelled anything (or anyone) that did not increase our profitability. I had been too lax in the past, trusting others to do the right thing. I had taken my finger off the pulse and could see that we'd become bloated, slow moving and lethargic.

I still had the tax issue, but something remarkable happened once those two traitors had gone. Overnight, the salaries I had been paying them (a total of $250 000) just disappeared off the slate. And when I looked at the clients they had taken, most of them were price-sensitive minnows that delivered next to nothing in profit. While the experience of having clients poached from under my nose was an emotional hit, the financial hit wasn't as bad as I thought. It was a bonus in some way. It left me with loyal clients who wanted the full, five-star service we offered and were happy to pay full price to get it.

I paid the tax bill, and resolved to only focus on clients who appreciated what we had, and to be more diligent with my hiring processes to avoid betrayal in the future.

The impact these new systems had on the business was incredible. For the first time since I went into business, I was now profitable. I had KPIs in place that made everyone accountable. I had systems that flagged when things were going off track. I knew where every dollar was going, what delivered a result and what was wasted effort. It felt good. I decided from then on, profit would be what I focused on; profit would be my goal; profit would be my yardstick of success.

## Profit is the goal

I discovered two important lessons during this time. First, I learned that being busy should not be confused with being productive, and certainly not with being profitable.

The other lesson was that profit is the only thing that matters. It's the *only* thing. I know that runs counter to the prevailing wisdom of the start-up community where revenue is the flavour of the day, but that's not the world I operate in. I run a real business, with real people, who make something that others want to buy, who pay us in real money, and then we do it all over again.

Sure, we'd all love to be the next Atlassian or Canva where we don't have to worry about making a profit every quarter, but what most novice business owners who idolise this investor model don't realise is this: once a start-up business owner takes capital from investors, they have a sizable gun at their head and that founder is running on borrowed time to deliver a substantial result to those investors.

We don't read about these stories in the Entrepreneur section of *The Sydney Morning Herald* because making a solid (but not stratospheric) profit is not sexy or sensational. It doesn't make for great clickbait. But running a profitable business takes effort, stamina and self-belief, so we should be celebrating those who make a profit every year, not just those who seal a deal to get a cash injection of $50 million off the back of a high valuation.

If a story that celebrated profit was written, it would read something like:

> *In breaking news, a man worked 80 hours a week for five years straight to generate a profit, and gave up all semblance of a normal life to do so. He was so worried about keeping the business afloat he could only sleep four to five hours a night. What did he think about in those dark nights of the soul? The usual things. Generating leads. Making payroll. Protecting data. Paying his tax. He worked his guts out, and paid his people a respectful wage so they could pay their mortgage and feed their family, even when it meant he couldn't.*

> *But he* did *make a profit and that is a story worth telling.*

# Your identity drives your actions.

# Chapter 6
# How to think big

I t's said, 'We are the product of the five people we spend the most time with.' I think that's true. That's why I really like living on Sydney's northern beaches. We have the world's best beaches in one direction, a tropical rainforest in the other and the riches of a cosmopolitan café lifestyle smack bang in between. We have the best of all worlds.

But what I really love about living here is that many of the inhabitants are as equally driven as I am. We egg each other on, hold each other to a higher standard and help each other to step out of our comfort zones.

For example, a beautiful super yacht called *Hey Jude* pulled up beside my boat at the marina the other day. It dwarfed mine by a factor of five. I had a bit of boat envy, but I didn't begrudge the guy who owned it. I applauded his vision and the achievements that enabled him to acquire it.

As I drove out of the car park, I wondered 'What would a boat like that cost? What would I need to do to be able to afford it?' That boat inspired me to think bigger for my next business and gave me a goal to work towards.

My wife says it's a 'big swinging dicks' competition, and there may be some truth to that, but I genuinely enjoy seeing others around me achieve their long-awaited, much-vaunted goals. I also learn a lot from seeing how they achieve it all. I haven't always been a 'think big' kind of person. In fact, I used to suffer from imposter syndrome and would routinely pull back on setting big goals for fear I would never reach them and then feel like a failure.

That was until I met Mudguard, the owner of *Hey Jude*. He runs an industrial concreting business. It's heavy duty, dusty, dirty work. He turns over $1 million a month, and has done for the past 20 years, and from what I can see, spends most of the time tinkering with his big boat. He's doing something right.

When I told him 10 years ago I wanted to sell my business for $2 million, he said, 'Kobi, think big—much bigger. Why not sell it for $20 million?'

It had never occurred to me that I could sell it for that amount. I decided that day to 10× my goal and to sell my business for $20 million. Ten years later, that dream has been realised and I have Mudguard to thank for helping me think bigger.

My new goal is to sell my next business for $100 million. By hanging out with people like Mudguard I am more likely to achieve it.

Just as Mudguard inspired me to set a big hairy audacious goal, I now coach my clients to do the same. I challenge them to think much bigger: to 10× those goals. If they want to build a $20 million business, I say, 'Why not build a $100 million business? Or a $200 million business? They say, just as I did, 'No-one has challenged me to think that big before.'

## Coming up with goals

If you ask most people what they want to achieve, they'll say, 'Um, not sure', or, 'Never thought about it', or 'Don't know'. They *do* know;

they've just never been challenged to think about it, which is why most people sleepwalk through life, wake up at 60 years old and wonder what happened.

People can achieve anything they set their mind to. If they say, 'No, I can't', it's because they're not clear what their goal is, which means the goal is probably not on their list, which means they can't possibly reach it. People don't fail because they're not good enough, or talented enough; they fail because they don't know what to aim for.

That's why my intelligent questions (IQ) checklist is so powerful. It helps people identify what they want and gives them a starting point for making it happen. I use it to help my team and clients think big and 10× their goals.

## THE INTELLIGENT QUESTIONS (IQ) CHECKLIST

These questions help people get clarity about what they want to achieve, identify what's stopping them from getting it, and determine the steps needed to make it happen.

There are seven questions:

1. In thinking about the next 12 months, what does success look like?

2. In thinking about the next 12 months, what could go wrong?

3. In thinking about the past 12 months, what went wrong?

4. And what do you propose to do about that?

5. And what's on your mind?

6. And what else?

7. And if I was to be giving you some kind of help, what kind of help would you be looking for?

Most people set their sights too low or don't set them at all, to prevent themselves from being disappointed if it doesn't work out. To break out of this circle of negative thinking, we need to set goals that excite us, that make us smile—that make us hungry.

# Achieving your big hairy audacious goal

Here are the five steps to achieving your exciting 10× goal.

## 1. Decide on your goal and 10× it

We need to set big goals. If they're too modest, they won't inspire us to take action. Most people think too small, achieve half of what they set out to achieve and end up disappointed. Think big, 10× your goal, and if you achieve just a fraction of it, you're ahead.

Big goals provide the 'carrot' that pulls us through the arduous task of completing the difficult tasks we don't like doing but need to do.

I have many unpleasant tasks on my 'to do' list—that's just part and parcel of being a business owner—but when I am fully connected to what my goal is and how those tasks will help me get closer to my goal, I find it super easy to get motivated and get those things done.

If my clients struggle to name an exciting goal, I say, 'Tell me about an amazing holiday you'd like to take one day. Where is it? Who are you with? How do you feel? What are you doing? How long is it for? How did you get there?' I then ask them to 'five star' that experience and 10× it up. 'What does that look like? Tell me about *that* holiday.' I ask them about holidays simply because it's a nice topic to talk about and gets them excited.

Once they've outlined their dream holiday, I say, 'Now we have to figure out a way to get you there. It's going to cost this amount, so you need this kind of job to pay for it. Let's work out how you're going to make the income to pay for it.'

If they still struggle to come up with a compelling goal, I ask them these questions:

- If you had unlimited time, talent and money, what would you do?

- What does the 10× version of that goal look like?

- How long will it take to achieve?

- What would it take to achieve it in half the time?

- What massive action would you need to take to achieve that?

- Has anyone achieved this goal before?

Now you need to apply this thinking to your existing business. Think about what you sell and then 10× it. For example:

- If you sell online courses, what would the 10× goal of that business look like?

  » Maybe you're currently selling to individuals. Think big. Could you sell them to schools? To universities? To corporates? Are you focused on Australia as your market? Think bigger. Think global. What other country could you enter into?

- If you are a life coach, what would the 10× goal of that business look like?

  » Maybe you're currently selling one-to-one sessions. Think big. Could you run group sessions, or offer online courses? Could you present your work at a massive conference? Who could you partner with to get in front of more people?

- If you are currently an architect, what would the 10× goal of that business look like?

  » Maybe you're designing residential homes and school halls. Think big. Could you design museums, theatres or multistorey developments? Why not write a book showcasing your unique business process? Could you create a podcast where you interview the world's top architects?

Go into your 'dream room', as Walt Disney called it, and start dreaming about what it would mean to sell your business for $10 million, $20 million, $200 million or more. What would that mean to you? How would that make you feel? What could you do more of? What could you do less of?

## 2. Write down your goal

Now you've got your goal, you must commit it to the page. If you don't, you're unlikely to achieve it. I write all my goals down in my Book of 50. I keep this book with me wherever I go. I take it with me in the car, to meetings, to the beach, to bed (my wife loves that). It rarely leaves my side.

Every idea, thought bubble, grand plan or minuscule concept gets captured in my Book of 50. One idea could be worth a million dollars. I don't want to lose that! That idea may not be something I can attend to right now, but by putting it in my Book of 50, it exponentially increases the likelihood of me remembering it and acting on it later on.

### WHAT MY GOALS LOOK LIKE

I break my goals down into 15 categories. This ensures that every aspect of my life is attended to. There's no point having a 65-foot boat if I don't have any family or friends to share it with. Here's what my current list of goals looks like for each aspect of my life.

| | |
|---|---|
| **Wealth goal** | $10k per day, $200k per month |
| **Investment goal** | Renovate the beach house |
| **Business goal** | Grow 'Start-up Investing' business to $100 million valuation |
| **Branding goal** | Write a business book |

| | |
|---|---|
| **Skill goal** | Learn to touch type |
| **Health goal** | Walk for one hour a day |
| **Relationship goal** | Have a date night once a month |
| **Holiday goal** | Go skiing in Japan |
| **Family goal** | Quality dinners with my family |
| **Education goal** | Study at Harvard |
| **Home goal** | Build a clifftop swimming pool |
| **Health goal** | Weigh 85 kg |
| **Spiritual goal** | Go walkabout in the Kimberley |
| **Hobby goal** | Buy a vintage Porsche 911 |
| **Friendship goal** | Have dinner with a friend once a month |

You can use these same 15 categories to get clarity on your own goals.

Now you've got some exciting goals to reach for, you'll need to work out how to reach them. To do that, you'll need to audit how you're currently spending your time, accomplish some unpleasant tasks and focus on the tasks that matter.

## 3. Map your actions against aspirations

In the lead up to selling my business all of the prospective buyers wanted to conduct due diligence, they all wanted to see literally *hundreds* of documents, many dating back to the company's inception.

It was an onerous task.

I had my team of accountants and lawyers working on it, but it still required a great deal of effort and time on my part. I can't deny at times I thought, 'This is not worth it. This is too hard. I'd rather be on my boat, or surfing, or having dinner with my family', but I needed to dig deep and complete it. If I didn't, I would not achieve my goal of selling my business for $20 million. That was the carrot that motivated me to keep going and complete the process.

When accomplishing difficult goals, it's easy to get distracted and lose momentum. It all feels too hard but that's because you're looking in the rear-view mirror at what's already happened and what it took to get there. You need to keep your eyes on the horizon, in the distance, and visualise that exciting 10× goal to pull you through.

## ARE YOUR ACTIONS MAPPING AGAINST YOUR ASPIRATIONS?

When clients complain that they don't have enough money to go on holiday, or buy a better house or send their children to private schools, they expect me to feel sorry for them, or to indulge them a little bit. I don't. I say, 'If you are not getting what you want right now, don't whinge about how unfair the world is, or how unlucky you are. There's a reason you're not getting what you want.'

'What, Kobi?' they ask. 'What am I doing wrong? Why are others less talented and experienced than me making more money and getting all the accolades? What's going on?'

'It's very simple,' I say. And then I ask them the magic question: *Are your actions mapping against to your aspirations?* In other words, are you doing the work needed to achieve your goals? Are you doing the *right* work to achieve your goals? If not, it could be why you're not reaching your goals. Here's a story of a client who had big goals but wasn't prepared to put in the hard yards to achieve them. This is how I helped him get motivated.

# HOW TO GET WHAT YOU WANT

Corey is a builder. He does fit-outs for high-end fashion outlets like Chanel, Gucci and Balenciaga. He wants to build a business others want to buy and turn his company into a $50 million juggernaut. He's currently got a staff of four and is turning over $5 million. He wants to move faster, which is why he came to me for coaching.

**Kobi:** What's on your mind?

**Corey:** I'm doing okay but I want to move faster and I don't know what I should be focusing on.

**Kobi:** What level are you at right now? Technician, manager or owner?

**Corey:** I'm a technician. I do most of the quoting, the ordering and the onsite work. So yeah, I'm still in technician mode.

**Kobi:** What do you need to be better at to move from technician to owner?

**Corey:** I need to learn how to read a balance sheet properly and know how company valuations are calculated.

**Kobi:** Why do you need to know that?

**Corey:** So I can understand the levers that drive value and then focus on those activities.

**Kobi:** What would you need to do to learn that?

**Corey:** I'd need to do a company director's course or enrol in a short course in accounting.

**Kobi:** Okay, so what's stopping you?

**Corey:** I'm not great with numbers. I don't enjoy them and I don't have time to enrol in a course. I am on-site most of the day, I go to the gym after work, have a few beers with the boys, come home, have dinner, play with the kids, have a glass of red with my wife and watch Netflix.

**Kobi:** So, you want to build a $50 million business, but you aren't prepared to do the further study needed to achieve it?

**Corey:** I guess so. Sounds pretty lame, doesn't it?

**Kobi:** No judgement mate. If you continue to not know how a balance sheet works or how to value your company, what will the cost be?

**Corey:** If I don't know how to make my business more valuable, or how to assess any offers I get, I won't be able to negotiate the best price. I won't even be able to brief an accountant to help me as I don't know what work I would need them to do.

**Kobi:** How else will it cost you?

**Corey:** If I don't know what I should be aiming for, I won't know what goals to set in place. I'll just plod along each day without a plan and it's going to take me longer to get to where I'm going. Which means I will have to keep working these crazy hours. I am missing out on time with the kids now. I don't want that to keep happening.

**Kobi:** That's a big cost. What are you prepared to give up right now in order to achieve that bigger goal?

**Corey:** Time with the wife?

**Kobi:** Wrong answer.

**Corey:** I know. It's the mates, beer and Netflix right?

**Kobi:** You can have all that, but not right now, if you're committed to this goal of building a business others want to buy. You need to be continually asking, 'Are my actions mapping against my aspirations?'

**Corey:** I'll enrol in the company director's course tomorrow.

Corey is on his way. Numbers are not his strength but he knows he needs to understand them if he is going to succeed. He needs to do something he doesn't want to do but he now has a compelling vision to pull him through and give him the motivation required to take action.

## 4. Focus your attention on that goal

I was motivated to complete the due diligence process to sell my business because the deal was worth a substantial amount of money. The carrot was attractive. But what if you just can't get motivated to tackle these unpleasant tasks, even if you know they are important?

I would say that you:

- don't have big enough goals or you don't want the goal badly enough

- have not associated sufficient excitement with what those goals mean to you

- need a coach to help you achieve your goals.

### WHY WE ALL NEED A COACH

I have a coach. My coach has a coach. Even Tony Robbins has a coach. If you're not getting the results you want in your life, you might need one too.

As business owners, we get distracted on the day-to-day operational matters when we should use our time and effort to increase the value of the business. That's where a coach can help.

## THE PROS OF HAVING A COACH

Belinda is an engineer. She owns a factory that makes carbon bike wheels. She's a technician in the true sense in that she loves building bikes, making them go faster and helping others discover the joy of riding bikes. It's why she started the business. However, she does want to sell the business so she knows she needs to do things differently, think bigger, and spend less time doing and more time planning.

The trouble is, when she walks into work on a Monday morning, she instantly gets caught up in all the conflict, crisis or chit-chat coming across her desk, which means nothing of importance gets done. In culinary terms, she's eating fried chicken for breakfast when she should be eating lettuce.

If she keeps going this way, she's not going to achieve her goal of selling the business. She needs to remind herself every day what she needs to focus on, why, and how to stick to her schedule. That's where I come in. I ring Belinda at 7 am every Monday before her workday begins to help her get her head in the game so she can start her day on purpose.

This is how our conversation goes:

**Kobi:** What's your goal for the business, Belinda?

**Belinda:** To sell it for $15 million in seven years' time.

**Kobi:** Who are you going to sell it to?

**Belinda:** To Acme Global Bikes.

**Kobi:** Is this goal on your 'to do' list in your Book of 50?

**Belinda:** Yes.

**Kobi:** What will make Acme Global Bikes think you are an attractive and valuable acquisition?

**Belinda:** Recurring revenue.

*I then ask her a series of questions.*

**Kobi:** Why is this important? What do you need to focus on this week to bring in more recurring revenue? Who's needed? What do they need to hear, see or do? What actions do you need to put in the diary to ensure these tasks get completed?

I also 'cycle' (forgive the pun) through the Intelligent Questions (IQ) checklist to keep her connected to her major goals.

Belinda answers all these questions, identifies the most important tasks and schedules those tasks in her diary.

We speak the following Monday morning and have the same coaching conversation again. These weekly coaching calls create a sense of urgency so that the hard things get done. This ensures she spends her week in the 'owner zone'.

Our coaching conversations give her and her team the focus needed to complete the key activities that will lead to a future sale. I also help her focus on the bigger picture, and what life looks like five to ten years from now, and then I help her build the bridge to get there.

## 5. Audit your 'to do' list

I audit my 'to do' list each week to work out what I accomplished and what is yet to be done. Auditing the list helps me follow up with myself and with others and is critical to success, as I need to ensure my actions are mapping against my goals. You can't have a 'to do' list and then not check back to see if the actions were completed. Auditing ensures nothing gets forgotten.

### FROM THE MINUTIAE TO THE MAGNIFICENT

The 'to do' list system won't work if you don't audit it. I'm constantly flicking through the book, looking at what I can get done, what needs to get done. There's a bunch of stuff on there at the moment:

- Buy a Harley Davidson motorbike
- Pay an invoice
- Book a crane

- Get my motorcycle licence

- Read the book *Deep Work* by Cal Newport

- Take a touch-typing course

- Take the jack out of my car

- Update the quarterly business plan

- Finish watching a Tim Ferriss video.

I'm constantly looking for the big, gnarly, uncomfortable tasks that are going to shift everything forward. I ask, 'What's the most difficult thing or task on my list that's going to help me move to the next level?' Rather than avoid the hard things, I rush towards them.

I use one question to determine what gets done first, and that question is: 'What's important?' The answer to that determines how I occupy my day.

## YOUR IDENTITY DRIVES YOUR ACTIONS

My parents were hard-working people. They had to work even harder when Dad lost the house. Even when they had money, though, they worked. It was what they did.

'We are workers,' my mum would say. She instilled this belief in us all from a very young age. To this day, I identify as a 'worker'. It's who I am, and it has given me a deep and abiding work ethic that helps me push through the uncomfortable tasks.

What's your identity? How do you identify? Whether you know it or not, it's probably driving your every action.

## IMPORTANT VS URGENT

Often, it's the important things that are difficult to achieve because they're not urgent. If they were, they'd get done because there'd be an external force compelling you to do it. For example, if I had a keynote speech to give next week, the pressure and immutable date would force me to get my act together. It's important and urgent, therefore it gets done.

What about an important but not urgent task, like learning how to touch type? That's harder because there's no pressing need and it won't make an immediate impact on the quality of my life. I have to be super self-directed to help myself find the motivation to achieve that goal. But I know that once I do, and I can touch type at speed, I can create content at scale, be quicker at communicating and save myself hundreds of hours in the long run. It's important and will help me achieve my goal of building a $100 million business.

And lastly, you need to schedule it. If a task is not scheduled in my Google Calendar, it doesn't get done. Once it is, it gets done. I live and breathe by that schedule.

## DO THE OPPOSITE

I love the TV show *Seinfeld*. One of my favourite episodes is when George tells Jerry that no matter what he does, nothing ever goes right. Jerry says, 'If that's the case, whatever you think you should be doing, do the opposite.' George takes his advice, does the opposite of what he would normally do, and before long, he's landed a new job, a new girlfriend and a new place to live. It's hilarious. I also use Jerry's 'do the opposite' strategy to help people uncover what they really want. When I ask people, 'What do you want?' and they say, 'I don't know', I say, 'Okay then, tell me what you *don't* want.' And they're off! They have no trouble telling me that.

I was the recipient of this strategy many years ago and it made a massive difference in my life. It was 2008, four years after I set up my process improvement consultancy, Simmat and Associates. I sat down with a coach to see what I needed to do next. He asked me, 'What do you want?' I was stumped. I really didn't know what I wanted. He said, 'Okay, what *don't* you want?' That was easy. Here's what I said:

- 'I don't want to be on the 'tools' any more.'

  I didn't want to write any more policy or procedure documents. I'd done thousands of them and just didn't enjoy doing them anymore. So, I didn't. I stopped doing them, delegated them to others and decided that I would place my focus on higher level activities. That was the beginning of thinking less like a technician and more like an owner and set me on my pathway to building a saleable asset. I couldn't write a procedure now if I tried. I planned my own obsolescence. If you're going to move from technician to owner, you'll need to do that as well.

- 'I don't want to wear shoes.'

  I rarely wore shoes as a kid. I grew up running around barefoot on the beach and on boats, so shoes were never a big part of my wardrobe. When I wear them now they feel tight, restrictive and annoying. It doesn't make me feel good and I don't like feeling that way. Today, I measure my success by the number of consecutive days I can go without wearing shoes.

- 'I don't want to wear suits.'

  I don't like suits either. It's what they represent. It means there's a meeting coming up; that I have to get in the car, drive to a meeting, deal with traffic, noise, pollution and all the crazies on the road trying to cut in. Symbolically, it means I have no control over my time, or the flexibility to conduct a meeting on my terms.

That one session with a coach set me up to think more like an owner. If becoming an owner is going to help me get less of what I don't want, then that's what I'll become. Now, whenever I don't want to do something that's difficult or confronting, I think about wearing shoes and suits and it motivates me to get it done.

You can use this process in a sales conversation. If the prospect doesn't know what they want from your product, ask them what they *don't* want. They've given you their objections so now you just need to present them with the opposite of what they don't want. Done deal.

# Act in haste. Repent at leisure.

# Chapter 7
# Management by walking around (the lake)

W hat did Charles Dickens, Mark Twain and Marcus Aurelius all have in common? They were all great writers but they were also avid walkers, and each waxed lyrical on the wondrous properties of walking. They were right. Numerous studies show that walking facilitates divergent thinking, a thought process that generates a range of solutions to a possible problem: that it irons out the kinks in a concept and helps create perspective and generates unusual or unexpected possibilities.

I stumbled on the surprising benefits of walking during COVID-19. I had a major decision to make, was stressed and couldn't think straight. I live near a beautiful lake so I went for a walk to clear my mind. Two hours and 10 kilometres later, I returned home, had a snack and I had the answer to my problem. I enjoyed the walk and the clarity of thought it provided so much, I got up at dawn the next day and did it all again. I appreciate the quiet pleasure of being up and out before the rest of the world has woken up.

I invited my brother Daen along one morning as he had to make an important investment decision for his manufacturing business and needed a guiding hand. I met him at the lake, we walked and talked, and he found the cleansing nature of the walk so stimulating, he joined me again the next day.

When the COVID-19 restrictions really kicked in, the only way I could connect with my management team was by meeting up outside. So, I invited one of my senior managers along for a walk as she needed coaching on a particular issue. She came, we walked and talked and by the end of two hours we'd not only solved that issue, but had generated a host of other new initiatives.

These strolls became so beneficial, I extended the invitation to all my management team and our 'walk and talk' sessions became a thing. We'd walk around the lake for two hours, I'd buy them breakfast and then we'd all return to our respective homes to start work.

The lake walk had no traffic lights or barriers, which meant the conversation flowed without distraction or interference, and trains of thought could be maintained. When left to walk and talk without limits or constraints, the conversation meandered into all sorts of interesting territories. People who may not work together or even know each other that well, find themselves walking in lockstep around the lake and talking about a range of topics they would not normally discuss. We know that the act of walking releases endorphins, makes people feel better, and unshackles them from the burden of their roles and responsibilities. But what we discovered is that it also allowed people to shed their corporate skins and to see each other as real people: parents, partners, sons and daughters. People with lives outside of work and all the associated messy complications that comes with being human.

Now we all meet once a week for a walk around the lake. I call it 'management by walking around (the lake) (MBWA)' in deference to the seminal book *In search of excellence* by Tom Peters and Robert Waterman Jr. Any leader worth their salt back when it was published in 2004 had a copy of it on their bookshelf.

MBWA involved managers wandering around in an unstructured manner, randomly checking in on employees, the equipment they were working on or the status of a job. Author Tom Peters refers to this as Managing By Wandering Around, a Hewlett-Packard 'secret'. The expected benefit was that by randomly walking around, the manager would stumble on what the employees were really doing, or talking about, which would help the manager facilitate improvements in morale, purpose or productivity. I'm sure the employees really enjoyed that! ☺

## Two walks, two sleeps: the ultimate guide to conflict resolution

Act in haste. Repent at leisure.

I hired a very difficult employee a while back. Unfortunately, I had to dismiss him as his actions and attitude were out of alignment with our corporate values. He didn't take kindly to that decision, so he decided to fight it out at the Industrial Relations Commission. Prior to the hearing, he sent my clients dozens of emails containing fanciful fibs and lies. He rang my staff and abused them, made a nuisance of himself in myriad ways and caused a lot of mischief.

This behaviour just reinforced my decision. I held my ground. I knew I was in the right, had not done anything wrong and that this disgruntled person was just trying it on. But it was very disruptive, upsetting and stressful for everyone involved.

Whenever I received one of his emails, or heard what he'd said to clients, I was tempted to jump on the phone and tell him what I thought, shoot off an angry email or get my lawyer to send him a threatening letter. As satisfying as that would all have been, the reality is that impulsive and indulgent behaviour would have just thrown more fuel on the fire.

My secret to managing conflict now is simple. When confronted with a situation that fires up my amygdala and creates the fight, flight or freeze response, I stop, breathe and step away from the desk. I take two long walks, get two good sleeps and then I respond.

This walk/talk/sleep method gives my sympathetic nervous system a chance to calm down, and helps dissipate the cascade of cortisol that floods my brain and causes me to react in harmful and unhelpful ways.

This simple conflict resolution method has saved me millions of dollars. It's stopped me from suing people (who didn't deserve to be sued), being sued (when I didn't deserve to be sued), sacking clients (impulsively) and sacking staff (inappropriately).

So take the time to get those two walks and two sleeps and I guarantee you'll see your problems in a new light.

Our walk and talk sessions are a wonderful team activity, a tradition that is fast becoming a ritual. We cover a lot of ground — metaphorically and literally — and the activity adds a vibrant depth and tone to the team. Building a team culture is not unlike building a friendship. It starts with spending unhurried time together, and what better way to do that than by walking? It brought our team closer together too. When you know what's going on for your colleagues *outside* of the office, it makes you more empathetic to what's going on for them *inside* the office. And that's got to be good for business.

# PART I TAKEAWAYS

1. Think like an owner from the start.

2. Hire people as quickly as possible.

3. Stop trying to do everything yourself and remove yourself from the day-to-day operations as soon as you can.

4. Before you hire anyone, ask the three key questions—do you get it, want it and have capacity?

5. Buy a notebook and list everything in it you want to do, be and have. Flick through it each night to create your 'to do' list for the next day.

6. Choose the toughest task, the one you really don't want to do, and complete that first thing in the morning. Everything you do after that will be a bonus.

7. Understand the love languages of those close to you. Speak in their language to build rapport and trust.

8. Think big and 10× your goals by asking yourself the IQ checklist of questions.

9. Write down your goals.

10. If your goals are not being met, are your actions mapping against your aspirations? Are you taking massive action to bring those goals to life?

11. Don't equate busy with being productive. Choose tasks that have a material impact on the profitability of your business.

12. If you need to have a difficult conversation or make an important decision, ensure you take at least two long walks and get two good sleeps before you do so.

# PART II

# MOMENTUM

**N**ow you've established your goals, dreams and foundations, it's time to work out exactly what business idea is right for you. A word of warning: if you want to make money, *serious* money, and create a lifestyle of the rich and famous, you *can* do it by pursuing a passion or hobby that you enjoy, but it may take you longer than you think and be harder than you ever expected.

Sometimes the most boring products are the ones that deliver the biggest riches, and a subscription-based business, the holy grail for buyers, can offer even bigger returns. There are lots of business opportunities out there, and in Part II I provide at least 10 hot niche-based ideas for consideration. Best of all, most of them don't require a lot of money, talent or skill to get started.

If you are to lead a team, deal with the inevitable crises that come your way and withstand the blow torch of being the face and front of a successful business, you'll want to know how to lead a team and deal with myriad pressures associated with being an owner. You'll also discover what specific activities you should be working on each day that guarantee your business grows exponentially.

Read on and discover exactly what you need to do to turn a small business into a big business.

Don't make your lifestyle fund your business. Make your business fund your lifestyle.

# Chapter 8

# How to choose a business idea that will succeed

'F ollow your passion and the money will follow.'

'Don't chase the money. Chase your dream.'

'Make your passion your pay cheque.'

Bollocks.

We get fed a lot of nonsense about how it's possible to make money from your passion. That you can do, be and have whatever you want and be paid handsomely for it.

That's *somewhat* true.

It's true if you're truly gifted at something and have a lot of luck; if you're hard as nails and can show real grit at committing to a difficult skill; if you have rich, well-connected relatives who are willing to help you along.

These mantras would make sense if we were all created equal, but we're not. Some people have more talent, luck, looks and money than others. You're kidding yourself if you think there's an equal playing field and that simply by 'following your passion' or even 'working hard', you'll level it. It's not that simple.

Don't get me wrong. I'm the most positive, ridiculously upbeat person you'll ever meet. I *ooze* optimism; it's in my DNA. I'm the last person to tell someone they can't do something.

But the concept that you can become a multimillionaire overnight from your hobby or passion has a few flaws and I'd like to point them out because this wholesale belief that passion trumps everything is leading people astray.

## Should you follow your bliss?

You can make money from anything but you need to work out how much money you want to make. And that comes back to the age-old question that I ask all my clients:

*What do you really want?*

If you want to make enough money to pay the school fees and take the family to Bali once a year, then choose a lifestyle business that exploits your passion and you'll achieve your goal.

But if you want to build a business others want to buy, and sell it for an eight- or nine-figure sum, you may need to do things a little differently.

Here's what I wish someone had told me at 29 years of age:

*Don't make your lifestyle fund your business. Make your business fund your lifestyle.*

*Then* you'll have the money to pursue (and fund) the lifestyle of your dreams.

# Why Jim Collins is wrong

This concept of 'following your bliss' was popularised in the 1996 book *What makes life worth living* by Gordon Mathews. Jim Collins took it mainstream when he featured the Hedgehog Concept in his 2001 best-selling book *Good to great*. Both concepts have merit. They help you identify your 'reason for being'. They challenge you to ask:

- 'What do you feel deeply passionate about?'
- 'What are you naturally good at?'
- 'What can you be paid for?'

These questions are set in a Venn diagram and the shaded section in the centre where they all overlap indicates your unique 'sweet spot': the idea you should follow, how you should spend your time or the business you should pursue.

The concept was updated in 2016 in the popular book *Ikigai: the Japanese secret to a long and happy life* by Francesc Miralles and Héctor García, in which the authors added a fourth circle to the diagram:

- 'What does the world need?'

# Do you want to be rich?

I have a lot of young entrepreneurs ask me for advice. 'What career should I follow? Should I work for someone or open my own business? What path should I take? What should I invest in?'

I respond with one simple question: 'What do you want to achieve?'

If they tell me they want to follow their passion and make money from that passion, I tell them to look at the Hedgehog Concept and choose a business idea based on those three questions. They probably won't be happy doing anything else. To *not* do it would not be honouring who they are.

If they tell me they want to be rich, as many of them do—especially the young men—then I tell them to ignore the bit in the Hedgehog

Concept that talks about 'What are you deeply passionate about?' and 'What are your inherent talents' and just focus on the 'Make money' bit.

I then say, 'Just go out there and find the quickest and easiest way to make money. Sell real estate, trade stocks, install air conditioners—but whatever you do, if you want to make a lot of money, don't try to turn your passion for basket weaving, making music or organic muesli into a billion-dollar business.

You'd be surprised to know how many supreme court judges and CEOs join rock bands, paint portraits or write novels after they retire. They've done the 'hard yards', made their money and now want to pursue their creativity without worrying about where their next meal is coming from.

Check out how Australia's richest people made their money:

- Andrew 'Twiggy' Forrest (mining)
- Lindsay Fox (trucks)
- Richard Pratt (paper)
- Harry Triguboff (property).

None of these sectors are inherently 'sexy' but they are seriously lucrative.

With the money you make from your boring but lucrative business, you can pursue your passion for making vegan glad wrap out of cornflower or build swags for the homeless out of beeswax, and you can do it all from the comfort of your clifftop mansion.

## Would you rather have been rich (and then poor), or never been rich at all?

I get asked this question a lot. The answer is easy. It's the former.

Life was great until we lost our home. My days were filled with surfing, sailing and swimming. When I lost access to that lifestyle, it made me hungry to get it back. It gave me a deep appreciation for the power of money and what it could buy. You can't truly appreciate anything until you've lost it.

That hunger to claw back the lifestyle I lost has never left me.

I did not want to be poor ever again so when the opportunity arose to make good money from conducting audits and writing policies and procedures, I ran with it. It was relatively easy, I was good at it and it was lucrative.

Do I love audits and process improvement? Not especially, but I do love flying first class, drinking fine wine and entertaining large volumes of people from the deck of my luxury home overlooking the ocean.

I was never bothered with how I was going to make money. As long as I could make it ethically and sustainably, I was happy.

## Sliding doors

I often get asked, 'Kobi, if you had your time over, what would you do differently?'

I would have studied a bit harder and gotten into the course of my choice, which was construction management, and I probably would have become a real estate agent with a side-hustle of building and renovating properties. My father passed down his passion for building and designing houses to me. A good weekend for me is building a fence, sanding or painting a piece of wood, or fixing the gutter. I also love seeing something being built from nothing, and seeing the joy that brings to people.

I would have made an awesome agent. I love every aspect of the job. Showing people through a house, working out what they need, negotiating the price, doing the auction. (I would have also been very attracted to the rent roll that came with selling those houses. That has to be one of the easiest ways to make money.)

If I really wanted to make some *serious* money, I'd choose commercial real estate. It's the same amount of work with 10 times the return. In addition to the sales commission, you get the monthly maintenance contracts for all the services attached to each building. All those fire extinguishers, sprinkler systems, maintenance panels, switches and fuses have to be maintained by someone. Add on the revenue from the insurance policies that underpin all these services, and you can see why it's the commercial real estate agents who drive the Aston Martins.

# What do you want?

Once you've established your goal and the business idea that will deliver you that multimillion-dollar pay day, you need to follow up with these four critical questions:

- How hard are you prepared to work to get it?
- How long are you prepared to work for it?
- What are you prepared to give up to get it?
- If you stick at this long enough, will you become a billionaire?

## Be realistic

Only a fraction of start-up founders ever reach unicorn status; only a fraction deliver their investors a 10× return; only a fraction get to stride the world stage spruiking their billion-dollar success story. There's a reason for this. Those start-up founders were unicorns themselves. They had unique talents, unique opportunities, unique timing, or all three. And that is why they have succeeded.

Take Mark Zuckerberg. He took advantage of being in the right place (Harvard), at the right time (2004), with the right people (Eduardo Saverin, the Winklevoss twins, Napster's Sean Parker and many others). Would he have been as successful if he'd been born

20 years earlier, and had grown up in Idaho, to trailer park parents? Possibly, but it's unlikely. Interestingly, Mark's parents offered to buy him and each of his siblings a McDonald's franchise to kick start their business careers. (He declined their offer.)

Zuckerberg and his tech bros were roaming the hallowed halls of Harvard, MIT and Stanford and mixing and mingling with some of the best and brightest minds of the day. That confluence of people, timing and talents led to the most extraordinary explosion of innovation the modern world has possibly seen.

Further, is it a coincidence that YouTube, Facebook, Twitter and LinkedIn were all founded between the years 2002 and 2006?

Is it a coincidence that many of the successful Australian start-ups we read about today—Atlassian (2002), Campaign Monitor (2004), Kogan (2006) and Envato (2006)—also got started during this uniquely fecund time? I think not.

Those early days of the wild, wild west proved favourable for those with an interest in the world wide web. The smart people with vision capitalised on that interest and the rest, as they say, is history. Timing matters.

## How to choose a business idea

So, what business idea should you choose? Where do you start?

Most people fall into something that they know or are good at. I did. That's how I became a process improvement expert. But don't do what I did. Do what I say and you'll get to where you're going a lot quicker! Be intentional, be purposeful, be strategic. Ask these questions:

- What do people need?
- What will people need?
- What problem do you solve?

- What can't people do without?

- Could the business sustain a downturn in the economy?

- What's the last thing people stop paying for?

- What business is least likely to be impacted by another pandemic?

- What business is most likely to benefit from another pandemic?

If still in doubt, start with Maslow's Hierarchy of Needs and work upwards. When times get tough, people focus on the basics: food, water, warmth and shelter.

Unless you have a crystal-clear idea of what you'd like to do, and the funds to launch it, start small, set up a side-hustle and see how it goes. Most importantly, get a customer to pay you for what you have! You only need one customer to validate your business idea.

## How to kick start a new side-hustle

Let's use the story of Nathan—the son of a family friend—as an example of how to build a successful side-hustle.

Nathan is 15 years old. He's in year 10 at the local high school. He sees all the rich kids get into fancy cars at the private school across the road. They've got all the designer threads, the latest phones, the cool haircuts. It makes Nathan hungry to do well, to make money so he too can have the finer things in life. He reminds me of me when I was his age.

Nathan came to me for advice. As always, I started with my key question:

**Kobi:** What's on your mind, Nathan?

**Nathan:** I want to be rich.

**Kobi:** Cool. What are you interested in?

**Nathan:** Minecraft, football and Drake.

**Kobi:** Do you think you can make money from any of those?

**Nathan:** Probably not.

**Kobi:** So how are you going to make money?

**Nathan:** I was thinking of drop shipping.

Nathan was on his way. I took him through my coaching process. He launched a successful business and is now a leading e-commerce entrepreneur.

# WHAT IS DROP SHIPPING?

Drop shipping is a business model in which an online retailer does not keep inventory of the products it sells. Instead, the retailer forwards customer orders and shipment details to a third-party supplier, who then ships the products directly to the customer.

In other words, the retailer acts as a middleman between the customer and the supplier, earning a profit by selling the products at a higher price than the cost at which they purchase them from the supplier.

# SEVEN STEPS TO BUILDING A SUCCESSFUL SIDE-HUSTLE

This is the seven-step process I took Nathan through that helped him achieve his goal of becoming financially independent before the age of 21.

## 1. Pick a product or service to sell

Nathan is an introvert and doesn't enjoy the verbal sales process. He already has a web development business and knows what it takes to sell a digital service, so he decided to sell a tangible product that he can see and touch.

Will you choose a product or a service? Choose carefully. It's a big decision. Here's a matrix of pros and cons to help you make your decision.

| Advantages of selling a product | Disadvantages of selling a product |
|---|---|
| It can be easily compared to other products. It is a visible solution to customers' problems. It is easy to describe and photograph. It is returnable. | It needs to be purchased upfront unless you use drop shipping or a similar method. It requires storage. It needs to be shipped. It can get damaged or stolen in transit. |
| Advantages of selling a service | Disadvantages of selling a service |
| It can be customised to meet a variety of needs. It can be discounted without it costing a lot. It doesn't need to be bought in advance. It can be delivered digitally. | It can be hard to describe to prospects. It needs to be sold by a salesperson. It can't be evaluated before it gets used. It can't be returned if the customer is unhappy. |

Which one should he pick? As Socrates said, 'Know thyself'.

## 2. Pre-sell your product or service to fund your business

Nathan used his social media accounts to promote his products and got some early sales from friends and family to fund the business. These pre-sales also informed his marketing strategy as he got an early sense of what products his customers preferred.

He also used YouTube to learn how to build a WordPress website, made $3000 building a few websites for family and friends and used that money to fund his side-hustle. He could have taken money from his parents, but then he would have been beholden to them and their guidance. He wanted to be fully independent.

## 3. Research the market

After conducting extensive market research, he decided to sell a 'white noise machine'. It's a three-in-one product: a speaker and a lamp that emits white noise and 10 other sound effects. He stumbled on the product when he was watching a YouTube video (about 'how to study more effectively'). The product is popular with parents who need help getting their newborn baby to sleep, and with students who want to mask external noises while studying.

The product piqued his interest so he decided to do further research to see if it would meet his objectives. This is how he did it. He looked at:

♦ *Google Trends*

Nathan checked out Google Trends[1] to see if interest in the white noise lamp was trending up, down or at all. He was delighted to see that interest in the machine had increased by 850 per cent in the last six months. (Why? Who knows. Nathan thinks it's because it dovetails in with the huge increase in the number of people seeking solace from insomnia, anxiety and stress.)

♦ *Amazon Best Sellers*

He checked out Amazon's Best Sellers (to access this tab, click on the sub menu tab 'Mover and Shakers'[2] and it will tell you what the top-selling products in each category are. The white noise machine featured in their top 10 best-sellers. You'd be amazed at how obscure some of these best-selling products are, how many are being sold, who is selling them and for how much. The long tail is well and truly alive and enables anyone and everyone to find their niche in the market. (Just make sure there's a market in the niche.)

1. https://trends.google.com/trends
2. https://www.amazon.com.au/gp/movers-and-shakers

- *SEM Rush*

SEM Rush[3] is a free tool that helps you identify the most searched words on Google. You then use those words to optimise your marketing content to increase your chance of being found online. Nathan tested different words and discovered that the phrase 'white noise machine' was far more popular than 'white noise lamp'. This was important as it informed his choice of URL and the words to use on his website that would help him rank high on Google.

- *Meta Ad Library*

Nathan also used Meta's Ad Library[4] to identify what advertisements were being used to promote the product across Facebook, Instagram, Messenger, Audience Network and other Meta products. The library showed him:

> » the best performing advertisements
>
> » the clients who are running the advertisements
>
> » how much the advertiser spent on the campaign
>
> » the campaign reach and metrics.

Why fumble around writing a Facebook advertisement from scratch when you can literally copy and paste the best performing advertisements on the market?

- *The App Store*

The App Store[5] is a great source for identifying what's hot and what's not. Nathan discovered one app for 'White Noise' that had more than five million downloads. He also found there weren't many apps operating in the sector, which is good news as it means the sector is ripe for exploiting.

---

3. https://www.semrush.com

4. https://www.facebook.com/ads/library

5. https://www.apple.com/au/app-store

- *Facebook Marketplace*

This secondhand marketplace[6] indicates what's selling and, more importantly, for how much. This site gives Nathan real-time prices on who is selling the product, what volumes they are selling and how quickly things are being sold. This will help him price his products accordingly.

- *Buzz Sumo*

Buzz Sumo[7] lets you see what types of content are trending, who is writing about the topic and where the content is being shared. Nathan leveraged this knowledge to get his blogs and social content into the hands of those who were already posting about it.

## 4. Choose your target audience

Nathan nominated three key markets who would be interested in buying this product:

- new parents who need help getting their baby to sleep

- tertiary students studying for exams

- insomniacs and those suffering from anxiety.

## 5. Test the product

Nathan didn't want to invest in something he hadn't tested, so he purchased one lamp from his drop shipper to check on the quality. This helped him see how the product got shipped, how much it cost to ship and the packaging requirements. Fortunately, the product scored well on every metric.

## 6. Build the website

Nathan knew how to build a website so he didn't need to pay anyone to do that for him. This is how he did it cost effectively. He used:

- WordPress as his content management system (Wix and Squarespace are other options to consider)

6. https://www.facebook.com/marketplace

7. https://buzzsumo.com

- Elementor as the website builder (or 'theme' as it is often called)

- Shopify to run and operate his online store

- SiteGround to host the website

- Go Daddy (or Crazy Domains) to buy his domain names/URLs

- Mail Chimp to conduct email marketing services and database building

- Draftium.com to help him create a free wireframe for his website

- Copy.ai to access free artificial intelligence bots to help him write his website copy

- 'Lead Pages' to create an opt-in so that he could attract visitors into his funnel

- an iPhone to take an image of the product for his website

- iMovie to make a video of the product for his website

- GarageBand to create the music for the video

- a range of free government websites to check if his preferred business names were available (if you can, try to match your business name with your domain names)

- Australian Securities and Investments Commission (ASIC) to register his entity as a Pty Ltd company (to take advantage of the protections and tax deductions a company structure offered).

Nathan's drop shipper also gave him permission to use his library of photos and videos to promote the product on his website.

## 7. Test the market

Nathan had a tiny marketing budget and wanted to test the waters before investing too much in untried strategies. Here's what he tested:

- *Influencer marketing*

He checked out the top influencers on Scrunch.com and Tribe .com to see what influencers could create branded content for him. He found three mummy bloggers who gave their endorsement in exchange for a small commission on any products sold.

- *Facebook Advertising*

He spent $20 in his first week to test his Facebook advertisement.

## Total cost to build a side-hustle

How much did it cost Nathan to research and launch his business? Not much. Here's the breakdown:

- Research costs: $0
- Copywriting costs: $0
- WordPress web build: $0
- URL costs: $20 per year
- Shopify: $10 a month
- SiteGround hosting: $10 per month
- Product cost: $40 for the lamp (test item)
- Facebook Test Ad: $20 per week.

Total costs: $100

## The results

In his first week, Nathan sold five lamps.

When he got a sale, he sent the spreadsheet with the customer addresses to his drop shipper, who sent the product directly to the customer. Nathan paid the drop shipper for the product costs and

Nathan banked the difference. These sales validated his product, price, place, positioning and promotion, and gave him the confidence to continue and invest more in the Facebook advertisements.

In his second week, Nathan sold 15 lamps.

Within three months, he was selling more than 500 lamps every month with a profit margin of $40 per sale, which generated him $2000 a month in revenue.

Not bad for a 15-year-old kid.

His next step?

His goal was to grow the business and sell it for a six-figure fee.

Coming up next: how Nathan used the Ansoff Growth Matrix as the framework for identifying his next move.

## Growth strategies for Nathan's side-hustle

The Ansoff Growth Matrix outlines the four main strategies for growing a business (see figure 8.1). Nathan's core product is the white noise lamp. He chose 'dried flowers' as his second product to launch. Here are the four strategies open to Nathan for growing his business:

1. *Market penetration*: sell an existing product (the lamp) to existing customers.

2. *New product introduction*: sell a new product (dried flowers) to his existing customers

3. *Customer acquisition*: sell an existing product (the lamp) to a new customer.

4. *Business diversification*: sell a new product (dried flowers) to new customers.

|  | Existing Products | New Products |
|---|---|---|
| **New Customers** | **Customer Acquisition**<br><br>Selling the existing products to new types of customers<br><br>(medium risk) | **Business diversification**<br><br>Selling new products to new consumers<br><br>(highest risk) |
| **Existing Customers** | **Market Penetration**<br><br>Selling more of the same to the same types of people<br><br>(lowest risk) | **New Product Introduction**<br><br>Selling new products to existing customers<br><br>(medium risk) |

**Figure 8.1**   the Ansoff Growth Matrix

Here's how Nathan used the four Ansoff Growth Matrix strategies to take his business to the next level.

## 1. Market penetration

Market penetration (selling an existing product—the lamp—to existing customers) was the easiest solution. He sent an email that asked his existing database to buy another lamp as a 'gift' for a friend. The email:

- cost him virtually nothing to send
- offered zero risk
- delivered a high rate of return
- generated instant sales.

He already had a steady stream of great reviews so it was a simple way to get new sales.

## 2. New product introduction

The second strategy was to offer a new product (dried flowers) to his existing customers. He'd done his research and discovered that dried flowers ticked all his boxes. They're lightweight, won't die, don't malfunction, have a similar target audience, are easy to showcase and complement the lamp.

This targeted a similar demographic to the lamp so it was an ideal second product to offer.

## 3. Customer acquisition

This third strategy enabled him to sell his existing product (the lamp) to new customers. His Facebook advertisements were on fire and delivered him an excellent rate of return so he just increased his investment in the media spend and saw sales of the lamp take off again.

## 4. Business diversification

The last strategy, and probably the riskiest one, was to expand his product range to chairs, linen, cushions and rugs. The products were all still within the homewares sector and attracted a similar demographic. He found new drop shippers to supply him with these new products.

Nathan went from a single-product site to a multi-product site. This was a big transformation for him but because he knew what he wanted (to make money) and started with the end in mind, he was able to future proof his website at the build stage so he could expand and grow as needed.

# Outcome of the side-hustle

Three years after launching, Nathan sold his business for $5 million to a homewares conglomerate keen to enter the Australian market.

It was a textbook example of how to turn a side-hustle into a multimillion-dollar exit.

Just as Nathan followed the Ansoff Growth Matrix to determine what he was going to *sell,* the global conglomerate used the Ansoff Growth Matrix to determine what business it was going to *buy.* It found Nathan's business very attractive for the following reasons.

## Customer acquisition

The conglomerate's existing customer profile was middle-aged, conservative women with limited disposable income and it wanted new customers. Nathan's business enabled the conglomerate to sell its existing product range to Nathan's younger audience.

## New product introduction

The conglomerate sold new products to existing customers. With an increased product range such as the lamp and dried flowers, it was able to extend its reach and offer new products to new customers.

# The bigger picture

In addition to the customers and new products that it bought from Nathan, the conglomerate was now in a position to become a dominant player in the Australian sector. Nathan's online presence gave it a competitive advantage, and enabled it to grow its database quickly.

When it bought Nathan out, its online presence in Australia was tiny and outdated. With Nathan's website and the infrastructure that underpinned it, it was able to get to where it was going so much faster.

The homewares conglomerate is now an attractive takeover for a company that wants to achieve the same result that the homewares business attained by buying Nathan's business.

## The secret of success

Nathan knew what he wanted from the business from the start—to make money—and he knew that the lamp would just be the first in a long line of product offerings.

This 'make money' goal influenced how he built the business from the start: from choosing the URL, to building the website, company structure, product strategy, and much more.

With this goal in mind, he was able to future proof the business to accommodate these new developments without needing to start over, revamp the site or change names.

It enabled him to build a business others want to buy, and it worked.

The secret of success? Know what you want.

# Not all subscription businesses are created equal.

# Chapter 9

# Ten hot subscription side-hustle business ideas

There's a reason Atlassian and Xero are valuable companies. They both have a monthly subscription revenue (MSR) business model. Your car insurance, health insurance and gym membership are all examples of MSR.

## WHAT IS A SUBSCRIPTION BUSINESS?

A subscription business is a business model in which a company offers ongoing access to its products or services in exchange for recurring payments from customers on a regular basis, usually monthly or annually. Typical subscription businesses include

Netflix and Spotify, but subscription businesses can also be defined as those that offer predictable revenue beneficial for both customers and companies, as customers get ongoing access to products and services they value, and companies get a steady stream of revenue and increased customer loyalty.

Almost any business can be subscription-ified, but not all subscription businesses are created equal. Don't rush in and choose a product just because you love it. Be judicious, objective and strategic. You need to think carefully about what you'll sell so that you increase your chances of success. For example, choose a fast-moving consumable good (FMCG). This means the product gets used a lot, runs out and needs to be replaced frequently. Think toilet paper, toothpaste and tampons. That's why the giants of the FMCG (Proctor and Gamble and Unilever) are worth so much. Their customer base is baked in.

In case you're lost for inspiration, allow me to present some subscription side-hustle ideas.

# TEN SIDE-HUSTLES TO CONSIDER

Here are ten non-software-based ideas to get the creative juices flowing. While software is a great source of subscription revenue, it requires a high degree of tech know-how, may take time to generate profit, and can be capital and labour intensive.

None of these ideas are new but they are reasonably easy to set up, can be customised for your local area, don't require vast amounts of capital and have a huge growth potential.

## 1. Pet supplies

Everyone's got a dog or a cat, and if they don't, they will one day. We have anthropomorphised our pets to such a degree that we now spend as much on them as we do on our children. As such, pet food, pet care and pet accessories are on a huge growth trajectory, and as the population continues to age and fertility rates decline, we will continue to treat our animals as human substitutes and invest heavily in making them happy.

**How to 10× your side-hustle idea**

Dog groomers are a licence to print money. Other than Jim's Dog Grooming, I am yet to see a successful national franchise leverage the significant opportunity this service offers. I spend around $100 per month on dog grooming for my little pooch. My groomer does a good job but he could earn so much more simply by asking a few 'would you like fries with that' upselling questions. Think of the logical services that he could offer as product extensions:

- dog walking
- dog food
- dog insurance
- dog flea medication
- dog accessories
- dog treats.

Most of these services could be translated into monthly subscription offers. With a bit of effort, a $100 monthly spend could be easily upgraded to $500 per month.

## 2. A cannabis and hydroponic store

Medicinal cannabis is here and the demand is set to increase exponentially once it gains mainstream acceptance. It's going to be a big money spinner for those who want to grow it and those who want to sell it. Why? Users will need an ongoing supply, they will want it from the same trusted source and they will pay top dollar to get it. Those growing it will need a steady supply of high-quality hydroponic supplies and sophisticated equipment to cultivate it, much of which are not easily available in retail stores yet.

### 3. Government tenders and contracts

This is a relatively easy one to offer. Most of the information you need to source is free, can be digitally transmitted and requires minimum customer service. The need for a business owner to know when contracts and tenders are open and closing is ongoing so the demand will never cease. You can outsource most of the research, automate the delivery of the service and easily create a system that removes you from the day-to-day running of the business.

### 4. Cleaning supplies

Hygiene will never go out of fashion, especially in a post-pandemic world. Cleaning supplies and cleaning services are both suitable for a subscription business as these services and products are needed on a regular basis, are commodities to some degree and people don't think too much about what they use, or who does it. They just want it done, and done well. Customers also don't like changing their cleaner as it takes too much work to brief the new provider so if you service your customer well, you should have a customer for life. Think of the logical product extensions such as house cleaning, car cleaning, pool cleaning, furniture cleaning, carpet cleaning, steam cleaning and lawn mowing.

### 5. Coffee

Who doesn't drink coffee? The consumption of this beverage shows no signs of abating and the need for personalisation and custom blends opens the door for small, boutique baristas to sell their personal brand to a wide range of customers. No-one likes to run out of coffee, or shop for it (it's heavy), so delivering it to the customer's door on a monthly basis solves a big problem for a lot of people. Commercial institutions, hotels and restaurants also have a regular demand for good quality coffee. Why not add tea to your product offering and double your sales?

## 6. Mobile car wash

This is a no-brainer for anyone who likes a bit of physical work and doesn't have a big budget to buy into a business. Similar to the cleaning example, car owners need their car washed regularly, don't like to leave home to get it done and don't really care who does it. You can grow at your own pace, open into new markets as the pace picks up and easily train up a team to do it in your absence. Combine this with the dog grooming business and your empire is practically assured.

## 7. Organic food store

Food safety and provenance has never been more important. Those with high disposable incomes or sensitive health issues will pay a premium for organic produce. All you need is a bit of space and some seeds to get you started, or you can buy the goods wholesale from your local farmer's market, box them up and deliver them.

## 8. Stationery subscription

As more and more of us work from home, the need to get a regular supply of stationery sent to our home will increase. Paper is heavy, hard to carry and needs to be constantly replenished. You can target schools and universities as well as the corporates and solo-preneurs to ensure you are not overly invested in one sector.

## 9. Accountancy subscription

Most accountants have a lousy business model. They charge us big time for a tax return *after* we've spent our money at the end of the financial year. What we really need is advice on what we should be spending money on *before* the end of the financial year. What's more, they charge us for every minute of their time, which disincentivises us to speak to them. What if they charged us a monthly fee that gave us access to them on a consistent basis throughout the year? It would smooth out their cash flow, and give them a source of predictable revenue. We'd get better value from their service and probably want more of their time!

## 10. Candle subscription

It's never been easier to source soy wax and wicks to make your own candles. People (literally) burn through their candles very quickly, which means the need to replace them is ever present. Buying a candle is not a grudge purchase either. People love buying them and will welcome a service that saves them having to schlepp around the shops to find them. If you can personalise the scent to suit your customer's specific needs and taste, you'll have a loyal customer base for life.

# Things to consider before you launch a subscription business

Here are a few cautionary questions to help you go in with your eyes open and make the right choice of side-hustle.

- *How much will the product weigh?* You'll need to deliver the product to the consumer and pay for the courier so try to pick a product that is light and easy to ship. You can pass the courier costs onto the customer but a 'free shipping' offer is always a nice way to get a customer over the line.

- *Can it get broken or damaged in transit?* If so, you'll need to factor insurance or breakage costs into the fee.

- *Can you make a buck from this?* Identify the product costs and profitability before you start the business.

- *Does it need to be packaged or packed in a special way?* Packaging costs for inner and outer packaging can eat into your margins. You'll need to factor this cost into your price.

- *Does the product work?* Before you launch your business, buy the product you want to sell and test it to see how good it is.

- *Does the market want it?* Pre-launch your service to build your database and validate if there is a market for your product before you invest too much in the business. There may be a niche in the market but is there a market in the niche?

- *Is the pricing right?* Pre-sell your service to check that the pricing meets consumer expectations. If it doesn't sell, test other pricing models and see what gets traction.

Don't let these questions deter you from getting started. Use them as a guideline for choosing the best possible business idea. Anything can work. It's just that some ideas are better and easier to implement than others.

Here are the other costs you'll incur in setting up a simple subscription business:

- building a website, product photography and sales copy

- website hosting fees

- payment processing fees

- marketing costs

- costs of storing and managing inventory

- labour costs of picking and packing the subscription boxes

- cost of shipping your subscription boxes

- customer service costs.

Subscription models are a great way to create a monthly reoccurring revenue model. Best of all, they can be built around almost every niche: from food to fashion to fitness. Check out the size of the existing community around that product or category before you launch and if it's sizable, chances are you can build a subscription business around it.

# Your team take their emotional cues from you.

# Chapter 10
# The leader sets the tone

W hat do you call a drummer without a girlfriend? *Homeless.*

How do you know when a drummer is knocking on your front door? *The knocking slows down.*

Drummers. Poor bastards. They get whacked around the head with jokes like these, but in all seriousness, where would U2, Coldplay and Red Hot Chilli Peppers be without their drummers?

It's a fact. All great bands have a great drummer. The guy who bangs the drum, keeps the beat and sets the tone. Without that regular drum beat, they'd each march to the beat of their own drum, lose their way and play out of tune. The result? Chaos.

I was a drummer once — not a very good one, but a drummer nonetheless. I played in the school band. There was a note on the pinboard: 'Players wanted'. I applied instantly. I couldn't play any instrument, but that didn't stop me from applying. I would have done anything to get out of the classroom.

They gave me the timpani, which is a big kettle drum. It's a deceptively tricky instrument. On the surface, the rhythms are generally easy and you only play two notes, but there is an awful lot of technique involved in playing these drums properly.

Having had my own business for 20 years, I've realised that being a drummer in a band is a lot like being a leader of a team. You keep the members in sync, on time and on song. Most importantly, you set the tone.

## Don't bring your shit home

My dad was a very calm man. He didn't get riled up about much, and he rarely blamed anyone for anything. Even when he lost his business, he rarely brought his troubles home (mainly because he lost it when the business went bust, but you get my drift ☺).

Mum and Dad now live close by so I get to see them a lot. One night they were at my house for dinner and had arrived before me. Fiona, my wife, and Harli, my son, were home. They were all on the deck having a lovely time, nibbling on dips and crackers, drinking wine (not Harli, of course) and enjoying the spectacular sunset over the ocean.

I'd had a really bad day. I stormed in, guns blazing, swearing my head off. Everyone went quiet, sipped their drinks and stared at the sky. You could say it all felt a little frosty.

Dad took me aside and said, 'Son, I know you've had a bad day. I know you've got a lot on right now, and I know you're under a lot of pressure. But before you arrived home, we were actually having a really nice time. Harli was telling me about his day at school. Fiona was telling us about your upcoming holiday. And then you come home, yelling and complaining, cursing the world and basically ruin the lovely evening we were having. Now, it's your home, and of course you have every right to speak and behave how you please.

But please know that when you walk in with that energy, it impacts everyone around you. It's not their fault you had a bad day, and by bringing it home, you infect everyone with your negative energy. Your family rely on you to be emotionally stable. When you're upset or unpleasant, everyone thinks they're the cause of it. If I can be so blunt, son, please don't bring your shit home.'

Dad taught me an important lesson that day. The leader sets the tone, at work and at home. I had an opportunity to put this lesson into action at work. It was just before COVID-19.

## Don't blame others —create a solution

I was heading to a meeting with a client. I don't like driving in peak hour and I sure as heck don't like wearing a suit and tie. But occasionally, an important meeting demands I do both.

I was halfway there when I heard a police siren behind me. I checked my speed. I wasn't on the phone. I had my seatbelt on. It couldn't be me.

The police car pulled up alongside me and the officer indicated for me to pull over. I was perplexed. *What could I possibly be doing wrong?*

'Sir,' he said, 'Are you aware you're driving an unregistered vehicle?'

Whichever way I answered, I was screwed.

'No, sir. I was not aware. This is a new company vehicle and I thought it was registered.' *It should be registered. I pay a team member a very nice salary to take care of this very thing.*

'Sir, I'm going to have to ask you to step out of the car,' he said. You'll need to leave the car here until it's registered. And here's a $1850 fine, plus three demerit points. Have a good day sir.'

I stood on the side of the road waiting for a taxi. By the time it came, I'd missed my meeting. I headed back into the office. I was in a foul mood. *Just wait until I find the person responsible for this stuff-up. I'll give them what for.* That's what I felt, of course. What I did was another matter. Dad's words were ringing in my ears.

I walked in, gave the ticket to the person responsible for registering the car, smiled and said, 'Please process this payment and let's chat in a day or so about how we can avoid this from happening again.' And I left the office.

I took a long walk by the lake, went home, had a good sleep and went into the office the next day. I met with the person responsible for the registration, told them what had happened and together we resolved how to create a process to prioritise tasks like this so that it wouldn't happen again.

Don't get me wrong. I was furious with this person for not registering the car. I hate getting fines (and the demerit points), but here's the thing: if I stormed into the office, all guns blazing, shouting and swearing, what impact would that have on this person and the rest of the team? If I was a gambling man, would I bet that it would make the team more productive or less productive? The answer is obvious.

Was it his fault? Yes. Did I get angry? Yes, but I was mostly angry with myself for not implementing a system that prevented this from happening in the first place. As a leader I can't always give in to the mood at hand and indulge my emotions. The question any team member subconsciously asks is, 'What have I done wrong to cause this reaction?' 'Nothing,' is the answer, but they don't know that and no amount of assuring them, 'it's not you' will make them feel any different. A team walking around on eggshells is not a productive team.

Your team take their emotional cues from you. As a leader, you therefore need to play a bigger game, be sensitive to the mood you bring into the office and keep the team on a steady keel. If you are upset, resist the urge to indulge in your emotions. Instead, ask an empowering question that sets you up to be the great leader that you are—or at least, aspire to be. You need to ask:

'What's the five-star version of *me* that my team need to see today?'

'What would an A-grade player do in this situation?'

'How can my behaviour be a ten out of ten for my team?'

Be that person! Demonstrate those behaviours.

It may not always feel good and you may need to check your emotions (and your ego) at the door, but that's what being a leader is all about. You don't always get to do what you *feel* like doing. You get to do what you *have* to do. At least you have the privilege of choosing what mood you bring to the table. Your staff don't get to have that choice.

Please note: a problem shared is not a problem halved; it's a problem doubled. Don't burden your family or your team with your work worries. They'll feel responsible and try to find ways to solve them, which will only make you more annoyed.

## The power of quarterly meetings

A leader sets the tone for their team, but they also set the cadence for communication; for how people speak to each other, how frequently they communicate and what gets said.

The underlying beat behind every successful business is the quarterly meeting. As the name suggests, this is a meeting held every three months. Like a metronome, this quarterly keeps everyone and everything on time and in tune.

We establish quarterly meetings with our audit clients, our coaching clients and each member of our team. The questions that get covered at a quarterly can be used for any cohort:

- What goal are you working towards?
- How close are you to reaching this goal?
- If you're not close to reaching it, what's on your mind?
- And what else?
- And what else?
- And what else?

Without regular quarterly meetings, the cadence and focus slow down, the team members lose their way and everyone starts marching to the beat of their own drum. Like a band without a drummer, the team can descend into discord and disharmony.

## The 90-day sprint

I often get asked, 'Why hold these meetings every three months? Why not every month? Or every six months?'

Like many of the most successful companies of our time (LinkedIn, Google), we also work in 90-day sprints. A sprint is when the leader establishes a goal for the business, allocates everyone a specific responsibility and then lets them loose to go and achieve it.

But why three months?

In the first month, the team unleash their energy and create momentum.

In the second month, they get focused, implement massive action and nail the goal.

In the third month, they slow down, get distracted and have forgotten what the original goal was.

Scheduling a 90-day sprint generates phenomenal momentum. It gives the team something to aim for, unleashes their energy and natural enthusiasm for reaching a milestone, and accommodates the natural slowdown that accompanies the achievement of a great goal.

## Not getting results? It's time to focus

If you already conduct sprints like this but you're not getting results, chances are you're not meeting with your team as often as you should.

It's vital you schedule regular check-ins with each team member. We check in weekly, monthly, bi-monthly and then have the quarterly meeting at an 'off site' event.

We seek feedback about the systems in use, and any points of uncertainty, and we share feedback on how everyone is going. This two-way communication channel helps re-focus the group, eliminate confusion and manage overwhelm.

If you can keep your head when all about you are losing theirs and blaming it on you.

Rudyard Kipling

# Chapter 11
# Be stoic

I got a phone call a while back from Jack, a big, burly ox of a man. He runs a timber mill in regional Victoria. 'I think I just killed someone,' he said, his voice faltering. 'I was driving a forklift and one of my guys stepped in front of me ...'

Another man I know had his hand amputated when the safety shield on the paper trimming machine malfunctioned.

A client who owns a security firm had to rush one of his guards to Emergency after the guard was shot in the back by an armed robber.

These are terrible situations for everyone involved. The injured worker, their family, the company owner and the entire organisation. Everyone is impacted.

When you work in industrial settings like these, as many of my clients do, it's inevitable that at some stage something will go wrong. After the police and ambulance, I am often the first person my clients call because they know that somewhere, somehow a process wasn't followed and they need serious help. Workplace manslaughter is a crime punishable by up to 25 years in jail. It's serious stuff.

When these scenarios occur, it's natural for the owner to panic. People are upset, there's blood, the sirens are wailing. It's chaotic. What I am about to say will sound incredibly hard-hearted and mercenary, but if you are the leader of an organisation and you experience a crisis like this, the best strategy for you, your team and the injured person is to stay calm, keep your head and control your emotions.

Yes, adrenaline will flood your body and cloud your judgement, but you need to stop, breathe and provide your team with the leadership they need to keep the company wheels turning. The team will take their cues from you. If they see you losing your shit, they'll lose theirs too, as you've just inadvertently given them permission to panic. The leader sets the tone and the tone you need to set is to be stoic.

Stoicism is not a quality people talk about much these days. It means 'enduring pain or hardship without showing your feelings or complaining'. It comes from the school of Hellenistic philosophy. Great leaders such as Epictetus and Seneca were followers of the tradition, as was Winston Churchill. He famously said, 'If you're going through hell, keep going. Hell is a terrible place to stop.'

When you are going through hell, it's tempting to think that now would be a good time to sell the business. It's not. Don't sell when you're going through hell. A business under duress is a low value business.

## Team comes first

When you step aboard a plane, the flight attendant says, 'Fit your mask before you fit your child's mask.' When it comes to being a leader, it's the reverse. You have to give the team oxygen first, before yourself. For example, if you take your profit out of the business before you pay your employees, you will be in a world of hurt, and possibly a court of law.

Of course, you've got to look after your own mental and physical state, and be good and kind to yourself and all that. If you're in poor health, the business will probably be too, but your team needs to come first. After all, what are you without your team? You're just a sole trader. They are the organism behind the organisation.

A business owner deals with a lot of chaos that an employee never sees, and nor should they. It's not an employee's job to provide succour to the boss. You may be consumed with worry about a legal issue, a product recall, a mandatory shutdown or a proposed sale that didn't eventuate. All of these things trigger strong emotions, but just as you are experiencing your own private version of hell, your team member might be going through their own private version of hell too. But is your anxiety worse than their anxiety? Is your level of stress more profound than theirs?

## There is no leader board of misery

When I was dealing with prospective buyers for my business, the due diligence phase was brutal. I had to provide over 300 documents, account for every transaction over the previous four years, read 130-page contracts with a fine-tooth comb and sit through extensive questioning from teams of lawyers and accountants. And they were the fun parts. I even had to track down the graphic designer who created my logo from over a decade ago to get her to sign off on the intellectual property. It was arduous, and very stressful. I did it all, of course, because I had $20 million riding on it.

Most of my staff were unaware of the deal being done. To alert them to it before it happened would only have caused anguish and upset. During this time, however, I obviously had to keep the business running, even though I was totally occupied with the due diligence.

The team, unaware of my emotional anguish during this time, came to me with issues that were important to them. For example, my sales guy Clive said:

'Hey Kobi, I'm really upset. My sales territory has been changed and I stand to lose $20000 in commission because of it. Can we talk about this?'

My marketing assistant Elena said:

'Hey Kobi, I'm really upset. The budget for AdWords has been cut. I stand to lose $2000 in bonuses because I won't make my budget. Can we talk about this?'

Here's the thing. Despite the fact I had $20 million at risk, Clive had $20000 at risk and Elena had $2000, all three of us felt equally anxious about our respective problems.

I had seven zeroes in my problem, Clive had four zeroes and Elena had three. But those numbers were all zeros so our problems were all equal. The problems we each faced had the same level of emotional intensity attached, so we all felt equally strongly about our problems.

I can't say to Clive, 'Settle down. Your problem is only worth $20000. That's not worth worrying about.' And Clive can't say to Elena, 'Settle down. Your problem is only worth $2000. That's not worth worrying about.'

Who is to say my stress is more than your stress? Someone is going to get stressed out from a negative comment on Facebook. Someone else is going to get stressed because they stabbed a guy in the head with a forklift. Relatively speaking, the emotional impact on each person could be the same. There's no leader board of misery. No-one's anxiety is worse than another's. No-one can experience *more* of an emotion than another.

So, when your team come to you with their woes, as much as you'd like to say, 'Jason, I'm sorry you got a one-star review on Google, but can you just go away off for a few hours and sort out your trivial business, because I've got bigger fish to fry right now?' you can't. You can say 'not now' and deal with it later, but you can't act as if your problem is bigger than theirs because it's not. You must treat their issues as seriously as your own, even if it is a low-level concern. The zeroes are all equal.

Show empathy to the team member who's suffering, be curious as to how you can help them, and above all, be stoic. Stay strong for your team, remain calm and keep moving forward, and you will get through it. You only fail if you stop.

If you really want to build your business, use the best part of your day to get the most important things done.

# Chapter 12

# How to work *on* the business, not *in* it

D
wight D Eisenhower, the 34th president of the United States, once said, 'I have two kinds of problems, the urgent and the important. The urgent are not important, and the important are never urgent.'

The Eisenhower Urgent/Important Matrix popularised by Stephen Covey in his book, *The 7 Habits of Highly Effective People*, was named in his honour.

Entrepreneurs often prioritise 'urgent' over 'important' because they are addicted to the adrenaline rush (the dopamine trap) that comes with completing something in the nick of time. But it's the important tasks that offer an entrepreneur the greatest rewards. The Eisenhower Matrix is used as a tool to help entrepreneurs overcome this common bias, as it factors in the *importance* of a task along with its *urgency*.

# The Eisenhower Matrix

Figure 12.1 shows what the matrix looks like. It's still in existence because it's still relevant and it still works.

| | Urgent | Not urgent |
|---|---|---|
| **Important** | **Quadrant 1**<br><br>Urgent and important<br><br>**DO** | **Quadrant 2**<br><br>Not urgent but important<br><br>**DECIDE** |
| **Not important** | **Quadrant 3**<br><br>Urgent and not important<br><br>**DELEGATE** | **Quadrant 4**<br><br>Not urgent and not important<br><br>**DELETE** |

**Figure 12.1**   the Eisenhower 'Urgent/Important' Matrix

## What tasks fall into each quadrant?

Technicians spend most of their time in Quadrant 1, which is why they fail to grow substantial companies. Owners spend most of their time in Quadrant 2, which is why they do.

Here's a summary of the activities that fall into each quadrant. Where do you spend most of your time?

- *Quadrant 1 activities:* important and urgent (*do*)
    - » deadlines
    - » last-minute tasks
    - » emergencies
- *Quadrant 2 activities:* important but not urgent (*decide*)
    - » strategy and planning

- » personal development
- » goal setting
- *Quadrant 3 activities:* not important but urgent (*delegate*)
  - » interruptions
  - » problems that are not your concern
  - » non-relevant phone calls, emails and meetings
- *Quadrant 4 activities:* not important and not urgent (*delete*)
  - » watching TV
  - » social media
  - » idle chit-chat with colleagues

# The 30-minutes-a-day secret to building a big business

Clients often say, 'I know I should be working on the business, rather than in the business, but I don't know what I should be working *on!*' So, how do you know if what you're doing is working *on* or working *in* the business?

If you want to create a purposeful life, you need to be thinking five or ten years in advance. You can't just turn up to work, sit at the desk and wait and see what happens. You need to be purposeful and work with intent. You need to audit your work from last week to ensure that each activity contributes to the greater goal, which is to build a business others want to sell.

What do you need to do *now* to enable that vision to come to fruition? What are the milestones you're going to set and the steps you're going to take to reach them? Most importantly, you need to understand the difference between urgent and important. People pay lip service to this concept but they don't fully embrace the behaviours that go along with working in the owner zone. If you're a technician and you want to move into the owner zone and work on the business and not in it, here's a five-step process for how to do that.

# THE FIVE-STEP PROCESS TO WORKING *ON* THE BUSINESS, NOT *IN* IT

Phil owns a crane hire business in Sydney's western suburbs. If you look up, you'll see some of his cranes in the Parramatta sky with his logo emblazoned along the arm of the crane. (You'll also see the Best Practice logo proudly displayed on all his vehicles.) He rents his cranes out to large construction companies for months at a time.

He launched the business because he'd been a crane driver himself and could see there was a gap in the market for a boutique hire service for high-end luxury development projects. He enjoys the business but he is stuck in the technician zone.

At the moment it's just him and ten staff, but he wants to build it up and sell the business to a large equipment hire firm. He tends to get sucked into technician activities so he came to me to find a way to help him get to his goal more quickly and with less effort. This is what I instructed him to do.

> **My goal:**
> Build a business others want to buy
>
> **Sell it for:**
> $....... million
>
> **By this date:**
> ...........................

## 1. Nominate your goal

Buy a notebook and on the front of the book write your goal so that you stay focused and on track. Nominate the amount you'd like to sell your business for (don't forget to think big and 10× your goal) and write the date by when you want this to happen.

Open the book and write:

- ◆ 'People' at the top of page 1
- ◆ 'Marketing' at the top of page 2
- ◆ 'Finance' at the top of page 3
- ◆ 'Systems' at the top of page 4
- ◆ 'Sales' at the top of page 5.

These represent the most important pillars in your business. Your pages should look like this:

| People | Marketing | Finance | Systems | Sales |
|---|---|---|---|---|
| .................... | .................... | .................... | .................... | .................... |
| .................... | .................... | .................... | .................... | .................... |
| .................... | .................... | .................... | .................... | .................... |
| .................... | .................... | .................... | .................... | .................... |
| .................... | .................... | .................... | .................... | .................... |

## 2. Make a general 'to do' list of all the tasks and activities that will help you get to your goal

Make a list of every task or activity you can think of that will help you reach your goal and then write that task down on one of the five respective pages. You may have dozens of items under each pillar.

Don't get hung up on what the task is, who will do it or how much it will cost—just write down what you know you need to do. Here's a few of the tasks Phil listed for each pillar.

**Phil's general 'to do' list**

| People | Apply for the 'Employer of Choice' award |
|---|---|
| | Write the keynote speech for the industry association conference |
| | Update the company policy documents on diversity and inclusion |
| | Clear out the email inbox |
| | Buy a birthday gift for the HR manager |
| **Marketing** | Create an online course to train up new apprentices |
| | Buy a new photocopier |
| | Write a blog for the website |
| | Launch an AdWords campaign |
| | Learn how to make a TikTok video |
| **Finance** | Move to Xero |
| | Hire a virtual assistant to do the bookkeeping |
| | Refinance loan on the crane equipment |
| | Find a new accountant |
| | Reduce 'accounts receivable' to 30 days |
| **Systems/ Data** | Hook the website up to Google Analytics |
| | Record a video of how to onboard a client |
| | Get a quote for new laptops |
| | Create two-factor authorisation for all email accounts |
| | Set up the intranet for online forms and OH&S |
| **Sales** | Write the position description for a new sales rep |
| | Increase the crane hire fees |
| | Renegotiate the sales commission with the reps |
| | Write a new script for the telemarketing sales team |
| | Seek out an agent for the South East Asia region |

## 3. For each pillar, allocate each task into the correct quadrant of the Eisenhower Matrix

Take the tasks you've written for each pillar and allocate them into the respective quadrants for that pillar. Here's an example of what Phil's 'People' quadrant looks like.

|  | Urgent | Not urgent |
|---|---|---|
| **Important** | **Quadrant 1**<br><br>Write speech for company conference<br><br>**DO** | **Quadrant 2**<br>Apply for award<br>Update the company policy documents on diversity and inclusion<br><br>**DECIDE** |
| **Not important** | **Quadrant 3**<br><br>Buy a birthday gift for the HR manager<br><br>**DELEGATE** | **Quadrant 4**<br><br>Clear out email inbox<br><br>**DELETE** |

Do this for all five pillars.

## 4. Focus on the Quadrant 2 activities

We know that the Quadrant 2 activities are the most important, so make a list of what they are. Here's what Phil's Q2 activities look like.

**Phil's Quadrant 2 list: 'important but not urgent'**

| Pillar | Quadrant | Task |
|---|---|---|
| **People** | 2 | Apply for the 'Employer of Choice' award |
| **Marketing** | 2 | Create an online course to train up new apprentices |
| **Finance** | 2 | Refinance loan on the crane equipment |

| Pillar | Quadrant | Task |
|---|---|---|
| **Systems/Data** | 2 | Record a video of how to onboard a client |
| **Sales** | 2 | Write the position description for a new sales rep |

## 5. Schedule your week

Before your working week begins, schedule these Quadrant 2 activities to be completed as a priority. Use the mornings to do the hardest work, the most meaningful work, the work that will earn profit. This is how Phil schedules his week.

He allocates:

◆ 30 minutes on Monday morning to complete the People task

◆ 30 minutes on Tuesday morning to complete the Marketing task

◆ 30 minutes on Wednesday morning to complete the Finance task

… and so on for the remaining two weekdays.

Here's what Phil's weekly schedule looks like:

**Phil's 'important but not urgent' Quadrant 2 list**

| Day | Pillar | Quadrant | Task |
|---|---|---|---|
| **Monday** | **People** | 2 | Apply for the 'Employer of Choice' award |
| **Tuesday** | **Marketing** | 2 | Create an online course to train up new apprentices |
| **Wednesday** | **Finance** | 2 | Refinance loan on the crane equipment |

| Thursday | Systems/ Data | 2 | Record a video of how to onboard a client |
| Friday | Sales | 2 | Write the position description for a new sales rep |

When Phil comes to work each day, he knows exactly what he has to do the minute he sits down. Best of all, if you follow this process, and spend 30 minutes on each task, by the end of the week you will have spent 2.5 hours working *on* your business, not *in* it. No matter what happens, or what crises come your way, you can relax knowing that the most valuable work was done first and that you are on your way to building a business others want to buy.

## Move into the 'owner' zone

Owners spend 95 per cent of their time in Quadrant 2. This is the 'dream room', where all the strategy planning, personal development, problem solving, self-care and goal setting takes place.

Try not to fall into the trap of getting stuck in Quadrant 1. It's filled with deadlines, crises, last-minute tasks and emergencies. This is what's called working *in* the business.

Ironically, if you spend more time planning and strategising Quadrant 2 you won't need to spend so much time in Quadrant 1 because you'll have fewer crises and last-minute emergencies.

## What's in my Quadrant 2 right now?

I am committed to learning how to touch type, so I enrolled in a course to teach me how to do it. I am all about efficiency and while I can type quickly with two fingers right now, it slows me down in every way. I need to get faster. Everyone needs to type, so I may as well take a few steps back and learn how to do it properly so that I can be more productive in the future.

# Do first things first

If you really want to build your business, use the best part of your day to get the most important things done.

Right now, as I sit at my desk writing this book, I'm pretty exhausted. I am in the middle of restoring an old boat. For the boat-ey people among you, it's a Halvorsen. I bought it in 2018 for $320 000 and am now restoring it to its former glory.

We took the wooden roof off to be redone and now it's ready to be put back on. It's the size of a small tennis court, very fragile, massively expensive and weighs around a tonne.

To get the roof from the factory to the marina, we had to get an 'oversized' truck to transport it, hire a police escort to protect it on the road, and then set up a slew of cranes at the marina to lift it off the lorry and place it delicately on the roof of the boat. It was like threading a needle with baseball gloves on. I was up until 3 am executing the operation with my team to ensure it all went to plan.

That's a long segue into saying I'm really tired today and I'm using the small amount of gas I have left in my tank this morning to do what I need, and that's writing this book. I have a lot of other meetings and presentations to prep for today that require a lot of headspace but writing this chapter for this book was in my Q2 list, so that's what got done first.

# PART II TAKEAWAYS

1. If you really want to build a business that sells for millions, you may need to follow the money, not your passion.

2. People make a lot of money from very boring products. Boring stuff can make you rich.

3. Pre-sell your products to check if there is sufficient demand. Why invest in a product no-one wants?

4. You'll need to decide if you'll sell products or services. Both have pros and cons. Do your research to ensure it fits with your personality and style.

5. Google Trends is a great way to test how popular an idea or product is.

6. Think like a buyer. Who would want what you have in five years? Build a business with that in mind.

7. If you want to make money, create a business that generates a monthly-based subscription revenue stream.

8. As a leader, you can't give in to your emotions or buckle when things go wrong. Be stoic, stay strong for your team and do what needs to be done to keep the company on track.

9. Keep your team accountable by setting quarterly goals, monthly meetings and bi-weekly check-ins.

10. Don't major in minors. Focus on the important (but not urgent) tasks that propel the company forward.

11. Schedule your day the night before and only do what's on your list. Don't let distractions take you off course.

12. Spend 30 minutes each morning on Quadrant 2 tasks to ensure you are working on the business, not in it.

# PART III

# MANAGEMENT

W e know that team, culture and management are critical to the running of a successful business. In Part 3, we look at how to leverage these three elements and the power of people to help you build a business others want to buy.

Wouldn't it be great if you could get rid of everything you don't like doing and give it to someone who does? You can. That person is your first hire. Learn how to hire that first person and you'll be on your way to creating a scalable, repeatable business model that buyers love.

Not sure how to assess new recruits? I've developed a foolproof, three-step process for putting all new candidates through their paces. Apply this process to every interview and you'll see the A-grade players emerge, the B-graders step up and the C-graders disappear. If you want a system for how to sort the chaff from the grain, this is it.

There's a little-known quality all successful entrepreneurs have that enables them to achieve off-the-chart results. It's a learnable skill, yet most find it difficult to master as we are hard wired to do the opposite. Mastering it will see you achieve success in a rapid time frame.

If you're tempted to go into business with a partner, think again. It comes with a range of headaches and handbrakes that can't be unseen or undone and can cause the business to flounder before it has begun. Discover how you can go it alone and be successful. Maybe you're already in a partnership? If so, learn how to deal with an underperforming partner, hold them to account and avoid arbitration, or worse, litigation.

Don't know how to sack someone, motivate a poorly performing executive or cut loose a difficult or unprofitable customer? Use the 'done for you' scripts I've developed over decades to deal respectfully, ethically and efficiently with difficult situations and difficult people.

If you want to build a business others want to buy, you need to build a team.

# Chapter 13

# How to choose your first hire

F or some technicians, the thought of taking on staff fills them with dread. Making payroll each week, dealing with conflict, managing under-performing players. It doesn't feel exciting, or bold. It feels terrifying.

But what if you were to look at hiring staff in another way? What if you saw the positive aspects, rather than the negative? For example, what would it feel like to wake up each day and only do the work you truly enjoy? What if you could spend your time doing the work that inspired you to start the business in the first place? What if you could give away or delegate all the tasks that drain, deplete and exhaust you? Would that create more energy, enthusiasm and excitement about taking on a team member?

If you want to build a business others want to buy, you need to build a team.

To make this next step a reality for you, you need to let go of the prescriptive notion of who and what your first hire should be. For example, if you have ever said, 'I should hire a CFO', or 'I should hire a sales rep' or 'I should hire an SEO person', you're coming at it from the wrong angle.

This 'I should hire ... ' attitude compresses your imagination and makes you feel that there is a one-size-fits-all 'first hire' for every business. There isn't.

# Doing more of what you love and less of what you hate

There's a much better way to go about hiring your first person. Here's what you should do.

### Make a list of everything you don't like doing

It could be:

- updating the website
- writing blogs
- speaking to customers
- sending invoices
- networking
- posting on Facebook
- following up sales leads.

Look at the list I just created. Which tasks did you instinctively shy away from? What filled you with dread? Make a note of them. They are the ones you need to delegate in order to move forward.

### Prioritise the tasks you hate the most

Out of all the tasks you don't like doing, make a list of the jobs that you hate *the most*. Create a job description for those roles and start thinking about who could do that job for you. You have to remember that someone, somewhere loves doing that work, is better at it than you and would love to do it for you. When you can find someone who loves doing what you hate, you have your first hire.

## Who should my second hire be?

That's easy. It's the person who can do another thing you don't like doing.

It seems simple, right? But few business owners approach their hires in this way—and yet it is the smartest and most productive move you can make. Don't make the mistake many technicians make and hire another technician like yourself. We gravitate to people we identify with, but that won't propel you forward. Seek out others who have skills you don't have.

For business owners on a budget (and who isn't?), you will be tempted to outsource some of these tasks to mitigate your fear of making payroll each week. This fear is understandable, but if you're to build a business others want to buy, with robust systems and people in place, you'll eventually want to bring these contractors into the business on a full-time or part-time basis. Buyers look for businesses that have solid, mature and well-oiled teams.

When you realise how liberating it is to rid yourself of tasks you don't like, aren't good at or that take too much time, you'll be delegating left, right and centre. Yes, it will cost you in fees or wages as you would have ordinarily completed these tasks yourself; but you'll recover those costs in the extra work your new hires will bring into the business. You'll also get to do the work you love. It's a win-win. And here's the thing: doing it all yourself *is* costing you already because it means you're not growing, expanding, building a team or creating systems—all the elements that make a business valuable.

# Aim to own

Without permanent, loyal and trained staff, you don't have a business. You have a concept. (Remember, outsourced businesses are less valuable to buyers.) This desire to 'own' extends to buildings, equipment, cars and electronics. I don't like renting anything. I'd rather own it outright. It gives me a sense of security and stability and sends a signal to others (and my subconscious) that 'I am in this boots and all. I am here to stay.'

Technicians have a lot of limiting beliefs about why hiring a staff member is a bad idea. Here are three questions I often get asked that reflect those limiting beliefs:

1. *What if the job I hate the most is the job that drives most of the profit?*

   Let me guess. You hate selling. Most technicians do. All that prospecting, following up, customer care, nurturing—they hate all of it! All they want to do is the thing that makes them happy: building, plumbing, wiring, baking, sewing, designing, coaching.

   But without a sale, you don't get to do what you want to do. Without a sale, you won't get to build a business others want to buy. Fear of selling is the number one reason why most technicians stay small and remain a cottage industry. It doesn't have to be this way.

   Believe it or not, there are people out there who actually *love* selling. They thrive on the thrill of the chase and love nothing better than getting on the phone and taking prospects from cold to sold. Yes, they are a unique breed—and they are worth their weight in gold. You can hire them to sell you, your products or your services and set up systems that take you out of the day-to-day running of the business so that you can get on with doing what you really love to do.

You are one phone call, or one LinkedIn click, away from finding that person. I set up Next Practice, my business coaching practice, to help people do this. The beauty of setting up a sales system is that once it's set up, it just runs. Yes, it needs to be nurtured and tended to, but once the systems are in place, the people take care of the systems and the sales take care of themselves.

2. *It's hard to find good staff. I've tried before and failed. All the staff I've hired have been hopeless.*

   Whenever people tell me that they have 'shit staff', the first thought I have is, 'No, you're a shit leader.' Never forget who hired those people!

   I don't tell them that, of course, but it's mostly true. That's not a slur on their personality; it's a commentary on their ability to lead.

   Leadership is hard and it doesn't come naturally to most people. But it is a learnable skill so there's no reason you can't develop those skills. I try to keep it simple. Communicate your vision, set the KPIs, diarise quarterly meetings and you'll be on your way to building a world-class team.

3. *What if I hire someone, spend a fortune on training them, and they leave?*

   Let me answer that with a question: 'What if you hire someone, *don't* spend a fortune on training them and they *stay*?' What would having untrained staff on deck do to your business long term?

   As an employer, you have to invest in your people, and paying for them to upskill is part of that. But you also have to realise that people have their own agenda as to why they work for you and why they want to leave. They move house, get divorced, want more money, need a new challenge. It's not your fault they want to leave. (Well, sometimes it is, but mostly it's not.) Shit just happens. People want to move on.

All you can do is try to provide the best working conditions possible and then hope for the best. What's the alternative? Never employ anyone because you're afraid they'll leave and set up in competition against you? I can't *not* hire people or train my staff for fear this will happen. (By the way, while this has happened to me, it happens less than you think. Most people are not born with the entrepreneurial gene. They don't like working for themselves and all the headache that goes with it. They are happy and grateful to have a nine-to-five job that pays them a fair salary and lets them lead the 'employee' life.)

If you want to build a business others want to buy, you need to employ people—and the sooner you do, the better.

The cost
of hiring
the wrong
person,
particularly
in a senior
role, is huge.

# Chapter 14

# How to recruit a world-class team

I won't lie. It's hard to find good staff, and as the global war for talent gets hotter, it's going to get even harder. The cost of hiring the wrong person, particularly in a senior role, is huge. Some say a 'mis-hire' costs 200 per cent of a salary. You don't want to get that wrong too often.

So, what does it take to attract the right staff? What do people look for in a job? Despite popular opinion, it's not just a large pay packet, flexible conditions and time off to attend a 'save the climate' rally. It's much more than that.

Frederick Herzberg was an influential clinical psychologist in the 1950s. He was interested to see what particular work elements made people feel exceptionally good or bad about their jobs. He conducted a large-scale survey to find out. The results were illuminating.

He found that certain job factors consistently created employee job satisfaction, while others created job dissatisfaction. He called it the 'Two Factor' theory. In short, there are 'motivating factors' (job satisfiers) and there are 'hygiene factors' (job dissatisfiers). To be an employer of choice, you need to offer both.

| Hygiene factors (job dissatisfiers) | Motivating factors (job satisfiers) |
| --- | --- |
| ☐ Company policy | ☐ Achievement |
| ☐ Supervision | ☐ Recognition |
| ☐ Working conditions | ☐ Work itself |
| ☐ Work relationships | ☐ Responsibility |
| ☐ Salary and benefits | ☐ Advancement |
| ☐ Job security | ☐ Growth |

Interestingly, Herzberg's study showed that if managed correctly, the hygiene factors could prevent employee dissatisfaction, but that these factors could *not* serve as a source of satisfaction or motivation. In other words, just getting the hygiene factors right is not enough. They will *prevent* dissatisfaction but they won't offer motivation and create satisfaction—and they certainly won't make staff stay.

# The power of the intranet

Intranet. Now, there's a word you don't hear much about anymore, but building the Best Practice intranet was one of the best business decisions we ever made.

As an accreditation specialist, I've had the good fortune to see up close what best practice really looks like in Australia's top companies. What they all had in common was that they had staff intranets, or internal websites for their team, so when I set up Best Practice I made that a priority for us and it has proven to be a wise decision. After all, if it's good enough for ANZ and BHP, it's good enough for me. (When facing an important business challenge, I often ask myself, 'How would a big corporate handle this? What would they do?' and then I try to replicate that in my business.)

My intranet has been an outstanding success. Every new hire we engage consistently tells us this one initiative has been instrumental in helping them feel welcome, educated and motivated.

## So what is an intranet?

For those unfamiliar with an intranet, it's a microsite for staff that contains a host of links, documents, videos, manuals and guidelines that show them who we are, what we stand for and how we operate. It's easy to navigate, simple to update and streamlines a range of business processes, such as onboarding at scale. It creates a consistent approach so that everyone gets given the same information at the same time, which means there is no excuse for people to say, 'Oh, I didn't know that was how it was meant to be done.' It's all there.

Creating a smooth onboarding experience for new staff makes a difference. A recent survey from the Society of Human Resources Management stated that, '69% of employees are more likely to stay for three years if they experienced great onboarding'.

Some businesses have a series of manuals that do the same thing as an intranet, but having it all online, structured in a modular fashion and optimised for mobile phone access, makes it easy for even the newest employee to find the information they need.

## Building a world-class internship program

We are a marketing-driven company. We create content on an industrial scale and use it strategically to generate leads, nurture prospects and convert strangers into clients.

As such, we need a lot of digital marketers to help us create and distribute this content to the world. The trouble is—and I mean no disrespect to all those talented digital marketers out there—there are a lot of 23-year-old marketing graduates who think that simply creating and uploading a TikTok video qualifies them as digital marketers. It doesn't. Digital marketing is a complex beast with many moving parts and requires a huge range of skills, some of which—but not all—are held by this aforementioned 23-year-old marketing 'whiz'.

I should know. I've hired a stack of them, paid them a small fortune and been routinely underwhelmed with their performance. That's my fault. I should have been more discerning. I am now. After too many false starts, I realised that I needed to teach my digital marketers how and why I want things done, and what real digital marketing looks like.

That's why I set up the Best Practice Marketing Internship Program. It's a 12-week program that enables the intern to come into my office, get a full back-stage pass to our digital marketing portal and get real-world experience. The entire program is housed on the intranet so the interns can access it easily from wherever they are.

Following is a snapshot of the framework we use to run our internship, what we look for, who we attract and the benefits it offers to everyone. You can use this model to create an internship for any division or department within your company.

Here's the week-by-week breakdown.

## The company induction process (week 1)

We know a clear onboarding process is critical for every new hire, including interns. As such, we make it clear what qualities we value and look for in a potential employee. When they log on, the first document they see is a summary of our corporate values (see figure 14.1).

1. Be on time
2. Have a good work ethic
3. Make an effort
4. Project good body language
5. Be energetic
6. Have a good attitude
7. Be passionate
8. Be coachable
9. Do extra
10. Be prepared

**Figure 14.1**  Best Practice's top ten qualities

The second thing I do with my interns (and more importantly, with all new hires) is hand them a bag of four business books, hand-picked by me, and say, 'Please read one book a week for four weeks.' They often look at me as if to say, 'Are you for real? Who reads books anymore?' (To which I would reply, 'I do. And if you want to work here, you will too.')

When the month is up, I ask my intern or new hire to tell me something they've learned from the books. I am not looking to catch them out or test them on the content. I don't mind what they tell me, so long as they tell me something. Believe it or not, I've had newly hired staff members, on six-figure salaries, who have been explicitly directed to stay at home for the first month of working with us and read the books, sit opposite me and say, 'I didn't read them.'

My head nearly explodes in frustration but I don't bother asking them why they didn't read the books or why they blatantly disregarded a very clear instruction so early in their tenure. I say, very politely, 'Thank you for your time, but we won't be needing your services any longer.' Their jaws drop, their eyes pop and they splutter, 'But … I thought you were joking … I didn't realise …' Too late. They are out the door.

That's not being tough or unfair. The 'read these books' policy is laid out in their employment contract (which is housed on the intranet) and they chose to ignore it. If they are so arrogant and unwilling to take direction at this early stage, there's no way they'll change their behaviour moving forward.

The other reason I instruct them to read the books is because I instruct my clients to read these books too. I need my staff to read them too so they are, literally speaking, on the same page as my client when we discuss key concepts.

This 'read my books' policy has become a very good (and fast) litmus test for who will fit in and who won't.

## Project work (weeks 2–11)

The intern now gets to play around in our 'digital sandbox'. Everyone gets excited because they can see what they're about to learn. And what a curriculum it is! Fancy being at the start of your marketing career, fresh out of university, and being told that you're going to be given first-hand instruction on how to learn all of the following tasks:

- Create social media content using Canva, Photoshop and InDesign

- Set up and record a Live YouTube video

- Respond to comments on LinkedIn, Facebook, TikTok and Instagram

- Create short videos using Premiere Pro for Instagram, LinkedIn and Facebook

- Publish social media posts using scheduling software

- Learn how to read Google Analytics and Google AdWords reports

- Write and design Google AdWords advertisements

- Learn and publish LinkedIn advertisements

- Learn and publish Facebook/Instagram advertisements

- Publish a blog on WordPress and LinkedIn

- Shoot and edit a TikTok based on current trends

- Analyse trends using data from Google Trends, YouTube Trending and Neil Patel

- Research, write and upload search engine optimised content for our website

- Present weekly findings to the team at our marketing meetings.

Any marketing or communications graduate worth their salt would be chomping at the bit to get stuck into this.

In addition to this training, the intern gets back-end access to all our social media accounts, the dashboards, the templates and the metrics so they can see how everything fits together. Once they have learned a key skill (e.g. how to film a TikTok video), they then get to make a real video, upload it, see how the metrics score and then repeat the process to make it perform better the next time.

### FORTNIGHTLY CATCHUPS

Once a fortnight, each intern meets with me or my marketing member for 30 minutes to go over the work they've created, the challenges they have faced and the next steps to take. The date is scheduled in their diaries in advance so that they know it's coming and can prepare for it. This is all part of creating the meeting cadence I employ with all my team members and clients. These regular catchups are critical. Without them, the intern can get distracted and lose momentum.

### Internship review and feedback session

At the conclusion of the internship, we conduct an extensive review with each participant and provide feedback on their performance. They provide feedback on us, too. We give them a written reference, access to all the content they have created over their internship, and if they are an outstanding A-grade player, a paid job. If they don't get to work with us, at least they leave with a strong skillset, a portfolio to show, a glowing testimonial and an education on par with a $50 000, three-year marketing degree.

## Saving thousands on recruitment fees

This hands-on, practical immersion in digital marketing not only excites the intern, it excites me! I get to see my content come to life, and I get to see the intern expand, develop and grow. It's immensely rewarding. It's also profitable as this internship provides me with a steady flow of staff. I don't have to pay a recruiter to find new staff either and I get to see them in action before I hire them.

## WHY I READ TWO BOOKS A WEEK

I didn't work at EY or KPMG. I didn't have an Ivy League education. My dad was not a corporate titan. I am a self-taught, self-funded, self-made man and have been since I was 15 years old.

This non-immersion in the corporate world has been both a blessing and a curse. A blessing because I didn't learn any bad habits from people who didn't know what they were doing, or fall prey to the old mantra, 'This is how we do it around here.' *But it's stupid and it doesn't work*. 'I know, but this is how we do it around here.'

It was a curse because I didn't have the direct experience of working under an amazing mentor or see up close the minutiae of how a big corporate operates.

When I launched my business, I did lots of dumb things that stymied growth, but because it was just me and I had no-one else to answer to, I could easily ditch a system and start a new one just as quickly. But this was a slow way to learn. I wanted to know what others did, how they did it and what I should be doing to build my business.

So, I had to source my own Ivy League education. My own Harvard. And I did. I found it in books. You know, those rectangular blocks of paper? Yes, books.

I now have an extensive business book library and I regularly turn to it to resolve a problem. Why wouldn't I look to a book? If someone who has made a billion dollars writes a book telling me how I can do that too, why wouldn't I read it? It'd be stupid not to. They've dedicated years to distilling their knowledge into 200 pages and I get it all for $30? What a bargain. The answers to my problems are right there, in black and white. It amazes me why more people don't read business books.

I choose each book for a reason. It could be a book about leadership, negotiation, sales or social media. In my day-to-day dealings with staff, I refer to the concepts outlined in each book and this creates a common language for the team—a shared ethos—and lets everyone know, 'this is how we do things around here'.

Importantly, I also give my clients a copy of these books as gifts so that they too know what concepts and principles we are following.

For the past 20 years, I've made it my mission to read two business books a week. I then take the best of everything I've ever read, synthesise it, make it my own and apply it to my business. It's like following a recipe. I am a trained chef and know that if you want to recreate a work of culinary art, you have to follow the recipe to the letter.

## Follow the recipe

Reading book after book made me realise that building a world-class business is like baking a world-class chocolate cake. You find the best recipe, you go to the best shops, you buy the best ingredients, you cook it at the prescribed temperature for the exact time and then you will create the perfect chocolate cake. If you follow the recipe, you will succeed. That's what recipes are: a proven pathway for those who don't know what to do next. And that's what business books have been for me.

For those of you tempted to mess with the recipe? My advice? Don't. My wife, for example, who is a wonderful person, is a terrible cook. Mainly because she doesn't follow the recipe. If she doesn't have cooking chocolate to hand, no problem, she'll bung in a block of Cadbury's Fruit and Nut. No self-raising flour? Plain will do. Out of butter? That Flora Pro Activ sitting in the back of the fridge since my in-laws stayed over should work. The result? Well, let's just say it's 'interesting'. (She is gifted in so many other ways.)

I follow the recipe because I don't want to have to guess if I am getting it right or not. If I follow the recipe, I will get it right. That's why I read the best books from the best business authors on the planet. I now don't even take a risk with buying a dud book. I only read books that have been referred to me by people I trust and respect who have actually read the book.

And by the way, just as reading a nice recipe book won't conjure up a gorgeous cake, reading a business book won't conjure up a conga line of hot leads. You need to actually *apply* the principles. You need to *do* the work.

## How to choose your clients

I gain a great deal of satisfaction from coaching business clients but I will only work with those who are prepared to *do* the work. I recently coached a man who ran a property development firm. I gave him two books to read before our next session. He said, 'I haven't read a book for 20 years.' I said, 'What the fuck is wrong with you?' I loaded him up with the books, sent him off and will wait to see if he comes back to me. If he does, we start work. If he doesn't, he was never going to take my advice anyway. Best to find these things out early.

# The reality is that not every new hire works out.

# Chapter 15

# How to sack someone (nicely)

N ow that we've covered how to hire people, it makes sense to learn how to sack people. I hate sacking people. It's one of the worst parts of being a business owner. But with over 70 staff on the team, 1000 clients and many millions in turnover, the reality is that not every new hire works out.

If you're a business owner with serious ambitions to grow and sell your business, as you grow your team of A-grade players, at some stage you'll need to sack someone too.

I was terrible at 'letting people go' when I started out. I held onto them for longer than I should have, even when the business was close to broke. I was reluctant to have that awkward and uncomfortable conversation because I know the impact a sacking has on a person, their finances, their health and their family. As a result, I take sacking seriously, and I do it as sensitively as I can. If I have to do it, I try to do it as quickly as possible, or as soon as the situation comes to light. You do everyone a dis-service if you don't.

I remember a time when I should have acted more swiftly.

# HIRE SLOW, FIRE FAST

I hired Shaun as our finance manager. We paid him an exceptional wage and had high hopes for him. He was a pretty fiery character but I saw that as 'passion'. He started strong and built good relations with the customers, but from the get-go, his team members (and many of our A-grade players) weren't too keen on him.

My Chief Operating Officer, whom I trusted, said to me, 'Kobi, you have to get rid of him. He's ripping you off. He's taking long lunches, disappearing for hours at a time, sometimes for days while you're away; he takes holidays without submitting the paperwork and doesn't reply to anyone's email, unless it's from you.'

I had a lot on at the time and wasn't in the frame of mind to deal with a difficult employee, so I took the easy way out and opted for the 'sacked but not sacked' option.

I said to Shaun, 'Listen mate, I need you to do the right thing, comply with company policy and consider our principle of fair exchange. If you don't, we're going to have to have another conversation.'

He said, 'Yeah mate, yeah mate, all under control. Been a bit under the pump, you know, problems at home and whatnot. But it's all good. No problem. Sorted.'

Nothing changed. In fact, his behaviour got worse. I confronted him and called him out on his deceptions, but he swore black and blue that he'd followed the processes to the letter.

The conversation got heated, we shouted at each other and I yelled, 'You're lying!' That was the nail in the coffin. Without warning, he stood up, leaned over the table, swung his fist and tried to punch me in the head! Were it not for the COO intercepting, I would have been knocked unconscious.

That was a sobering moment.

It was clear this guy wasn't just incompetent, he was a lunatic! I can hold my own in a bar room brawl, but I wasn't expecting it in my own office! Looking back, I should have sacked him when my COO first alerted me to his dishonest and deceptive dealings.

I've since learned a few strategies for how to sack someone quickly (yet nicely) and minimise the hurt and pain inflicted on the affected employee. It has taken me decades to refine this process. Like most things, it's not what you do, it's how you do it. For me, it comes down to how I manage the conversation. I have a script I use. It's not perfect and it won't work for every scenario but it's served me well over the years.

# Using the right approach

Before I reveal my 'how to sack someone' script, let me add a few caveats that underpin my approach.

## Let go of ego

Being right indulges my ego and makes me feel good, but it may not make me happy. For example, I could sack an employee, tell them exactly what I think, rant and rave about their bad behaviour, frog march them to the exit, throw them out and shout, 'You're fired!' How satisfying would that feel? But the result? They'll feel humiliated, disaffected and disgruntled. When they calm down, they'll probably ring their lawyer faster than green grass through a goose. Next thing I know, I've got an expensive court case on my hands. Brilliant. Just what I don't need.

When I have to sack someone, I don't need to be right for the sake of my ego. I just need the situation to be dealt with as quickly and as sensitively as possible so that we can all move on.

### Take (some of) the blame

When you read my script, you'll notice I take a lot of the blame for why things went wrong. Am I to blame? Yes, partly. For me, fault is like a pizza. There are slices of blame. The question is, how many slices belong to me? One? Four? It's rarely six but it's never none. I am always somewhat to blame for an employee not working out because I hired them in the first place. I make a point of mentioning this to the affected employee because when I do, it instantly puts them at ease. Not *a lot* at ease, I should add, as they are about to be sacked, but it does soften the blow, take the heat out of the situation and minimise their humiliation. It also enables my message to be heard. When people get defensive, they stop listening. If I can't be heard, the situation can't be resolved.

My goal is to deliver the news as sensitively as I can and get them out the door as delicately and quickly as possible.

### Be vulnerable

This script is not for everyone.

If you have a big ego and can't admit to being wrong, it's not for you.

If you can't say sorry, like The Fonz from the television series *Happy Days* never could, it's not for you.

If you can't show vulnerability and humility, it's not for you.

But hey, like my dad said, 'Do you want to be right, or do you want to be happy?' Personally, I prefer the latter. If you do too, then take a look at the following script. I think it's gold!

# What to say when you need to sack someone

Now to my 'how to sack someone' script.

Here's how the original sacking conversation with Shaun should have unfolded, before it got heated and ended in fisticuffs.

---

Hey Shaun, I need to have a difficult conversation with you. I'm not very good at having these kinds of conversations so I may not get it right. I started this company from scratch and didn't have a boss to coach me or train me on how to have conversations like this. I'm just trying to figure it out as I go. I apologise if I get this wrong and unnecessarily upset you, but I need to get this off my chest.

The reality is that it's not working out from my side. I laid out my expectations of the results we were seeking from you when you started. I acknowledge that they may not have been the best, or the right, expectations. Nonetheless, they were my expectations. You know my principles of fair exchange in that I'm giving you money for your time and activities, and right now, based on your last three months here, I'm not happy with what I'm getting in return for my money.

I'm not telling you that you *must* do these things, but what I am saying is that if you want to continue to take my money and that of the organisation, then you do need to complete those activities to the standard I have outlined. If you don't want to do those things, and you don't want to take my money any more, we need to work out how we're going to part company.

---

I've found this process works better than most because it puts me in a vulnerable position, acknowledges that I don't know what I'm doing, that it's hard for us both and that while they may not like the solution I am offering, it is nonetheless a fair and equitable solution that no-one could argue with.

## The cost of procrastination

They say that once you know better, you do better. Now I know better, I do better and I don't leave it too long to move C-grade players out. It's costly all round to hold onto them. It undercuts the value that hard-working A-grade players put in; it sends a signal that you tolerate bad behaviour; it demotivates everyone from caring about doing better, ('Why should I give a toss when people like that don't even get pulled up?') When you see bad behaviour, or even a hint of it, you can't delay. You have to get rid of that person.

# Fair exchange

The concept and underlying logic of 'fair exchange' helps transform an uncomfortable dialogue into a rational debate. When you present the staff member with the job description that they agreed to, and then compare and contrast it with their actual performance, it's hard for them to rebut the facts.

If I have to sack someone, my goal is to be as fair and objective as possible. It's also my responsibility to be prepared and to know what the position description contains so that I can assess their performance fairly. My core principles help guide me to achieve this outcome.

Many companies pay lip service to the concept of corporate values. They put a mission statement on the wall and never look at it again. That's not how we operate. My core principles are at the centre of everything we do. If you look closely at the script, you'll notice that my core principles are seeded throughout. The script is based on:

- *empathy:* I acknowledge that this information will be hard for them to hear

- *curiosity:* I give them the option to tell me why they are unwilling to commit to the principle of fair exchange

- *friendliness:* I approach the conversation with minimal ego, a warm demeanour and a genuine desire to be honest about my shortcomings and how I've played a role in the situation.

# What about due process?

It goes without saying that this script needs to be discussed with your HR person and your legal counsel. Every sacking needs to adhere to the rule of law (and there are many, many laws surrounding this), so before you go ahead and sack anyone, get your ducks in a row, get the script approved and if necessary, ask your HR manager and legal counsel to be in the room to witness the proceedings. (And if you've hired people like Shaun, and need to sack them, you may want a bouncer in the room as well.)

Neutralise their defences, counter with curiosity and engage with empathy.

# Chapter 16

# How to manage an under-performing executive

'We need to chat.'

These four words send shivers up the spine of middle management executives (and husbands) across the globe. The subtext is universally understood. It's code for, 'I'm not very happy with you and I'm about to tell you why.' Just hearing those words uttered can have a visceral impact on the body. We tense up, look for an escape and will say or do whatever it takes to get out of that situation.

If you need to 'have a chat' with someone about their under-whelming performance, don't kick off the conversation with those four words. It won't end well. So, how should you start a difficult conversation with a staff member?

How you frame it makes all the difference. Done poorly, the offending employee will take exception to the accusations and possibly seek legal advice from the Fair Work Commission, contact Consumer Affairs, or worse, *A Current Affair,* and make your life a costly nightmare.

Done well, the person will commit to improve their performance, or resign on the spot, with zero friction, say 'sorry' for being a bother and help you find a replacement. It's all in the way you start the conversation. For this method to succeed, you need to think like an army general: neutralise their defences, counter with curiosity and engage with empathy. It also requires you to take full responsibility for what happened. Whatever you do, don't attack. They'll get defensive, and when they get defensive, they stop listening. When they stop listening, you've lost.

Steve was a top-notch salesman. He approached me at an industry conference and said, 'I want to work for your company. I can do great things for you.' I was flattered but wasn't sure we needed him and told him as much. But he kept on at me, so I said, 'Come on as a contractor and we'll see how it goes.'

He said, 'I will get better results if you make me a full-time employee.' I resisted further but he, being a great salesman, wore me down. Eventually I said, 'Okay, let's split the difference. Come on board as a part-time employee,' and he agreed.

Just as he was about to sign the contract, he said, 'I'd much rather be a full-time employee.'

I said, 'That's not part of the agreement,' but he beat me down again with a raft of reasons why it would be a great idea. I was under the pump and dealing with other matters at the time, so against my better judgement, I hired him.

After six months, it was evident things were not working. My intuition had been right. I needed to have that uncomfortable conversation. I had two options. I could start with the dreaded four-word option—'We need to chat'—and set off his fight, flight or freeze response. Or I could use my 'It's my fault' spiel and hope he could see my point of view about why this relationship needed to end.

I plotted the script for both options.

Here's the script for option #1, the 'We need to chat' version.

---

Steve. We need to chat. The business has had a downturn, there's a lot of uncertainty in the economy at the moment and I can't afford to keep you on. As head of business development, what I had hoped to see from you was a hyperactive response to the downturn in conditions. I expected you to go in hard, rally the troops, put in the long hours and do what was needed to be the rainmaker you promised you'd be. But you backed off, accepted the status quo and knocked off early most days. You're a senior manager. You get paid more than me. My expectations were clear and you failed to meet them. It's time for you to leave the company.

---

Here's the script for option #2, the 'It's my fault' version.

> Hey Steve, I need to let you know that I've fucked up with something. I'm really sorry. My intuition said that I should have put you on as a contractor, but I went against that and gave you a chance to see if you could prove my intuition wrong. And how I've stuffed up is that I misled you at the beginning by not revealing the misgiving I had. I do the hiring and I do the firing here. I gave you the targets to hit but I didn't hold you accountable. I'd like to apologise for making this mistake. I shouldn't have brought you on, because that has built up your expectations and you've built a life around that. You may have bought a house, or a car, and now I can't follow through on that expectation and that's going to be difficult for you. I have changed my mind with regards to your employment conditions. You can continue to work here but it will be based on 100 per cent commission. I'm not going to pay you any base. Can that arrangement work for you?

Would it have been satisfying to run with script #1? You bet. It would have felt gooood. Steve had failed on every available metric, and he had cost me a small fortune in wages and foregone sales.

Did I run with script #2? Yes, I did because I wanted to be happy, not right, and I knew Steve was the kind of guy who would use the court to fight his battles and I certainly did not want that. He didn't love what I had to say, but he didn't get defensive, which meant he was listening. After muttering a few expletives, he said, 'Okay, fine. I don't want to be here then.' And I said, 'Great.' His response told me everything I needed to know about him. In effect, he said, 'I am not going to back myself on this. I don't believe I can deliver.'

He got what he wanted, which was a pay slip so he could refinance a mortgage, so I didn't feel too bad about moving him on. He was a masterful salesperson. It's a shame he couldn't muster up a few sales for us.

# Not all clients are created equal.

# Chapter 17
# How to fire a customer or supplier (nicely)

J
ust as staff can be under-performers, so too can clients and suppliers.

## Firing a client

Not all clients are created equal. Some are more valuable, nicer or easier to work with than others. We all know that 80 per cent of our business comes from 20 per cent of our customers so as your business grows and you become more discerning about who you work with, you will eventually need to cull a customer or two. It can be done nicely without hurting anyone's feelings or leaving you open to receiving negative reviews.

Here's the script I use to move clients on.

> Hi Bob, I need to have an uncomfortable conversation with you with regard to the future. I take 100 per cent responsibility for delivering the services to my clients and creating value. Unfortunately, we have not been able to help you achieve the benefits that you anticipated. It would be unethical of me to continue to take any more money from you. I can't deliver the level of service to the standard and expectations you have, so I will be withdrawing. I wish you all the best.

Here's a script you can use when you agreed to work for a set fee and that fee no longer generates the required profit.

> Hi Celia, I need to have an uncomfortable conversation with you with regard to the future. This is my error and I take 100 per cent responsibility for this situation. In short, I should never have accepted or offered the price that I did. I can't continue at that price point or I'll go out of business. I can't deliver the level of service for the fee that was agreed, so I will be withdrawing. I wish you all the best.

# Firing a supplier

I am restoring a beautiful old Halvorsen wooden boat. It's a thing of beauty. I can idle away hours at the marina just polishing and varnishing it, and admiring her from afar. I hired a crew of contractors to help me restore her but unfortunately, the work they did was not up to scratch. I gave them numerous opportunities to rectify the situation but they did not respond.

This is the script I used to fire them.

> Hey guys, I'm 100 per cent to blame for this situation. I asked you to do the work, and I let you do it to a poor standard, and I permitted that to go on for too long. I should have pulled you up earlier and now it's out of control. It's my fault, because I don't like uncomfortable conversations and I should have addressed this weeks ago, so now I have to take control. As a result, you're not going to be doing any more work for me. I wish you all the best.

## When in doubt, do nothing

If it's a super serious conflict or it's a situation that you don't know how to handle, the first thing you should do is nothing: do not react, respond, email back, ring them up or send a text. You may feel like doing all of those, but just know that conflict is rarely resolved over an electronic device. It requires a face-to-face conversation. That is a difficult ask for many people, especially introverts or highly sensitive people, but it's the only way, unless you want to escalate the situation and end up in litigation. Obviously, these kinds of difficult conversations can get messy quickly, so you need to have your ducks in a row before you start the discussion, and you need to be in the right headspace to confront the situation. (Before I enter any uncomfortable situation or deal with a conflict, I apply my 'two walks/two sleeps' policy to ensure I approach it with the right attitude.)

I always start from the premise that I am 100 per cent responsible for the conflict that has occurred. I assume it's my fault and start from there. Obviously, it's not *all* my fault but I act as if it is.

What's the alternative approach? If you tell them what an idiot they are and why they're wrong, they will bite back, and you will end up fighting on the front lawn or on the steps of the Supreme Court. I've saved literally tens of thousands of dollars on legal fees simply by saying 'sorry', taking responsibility and copping a bit of heat. I would rather be happy than right.

This strategy of taking full responsibility is not for everyone. You must leave your ego at the door, swallow your pride and stare humiliation in the face. Often, when I take this position, the business owner comes back with, 'Well Kobi, it's not *all* your fault. I was *partly* to blame as well.' Then you have a nice debate over whose fault it *wasn't*, and by the end, each party takes a proportional slice of the blame, which is much better than having an argument in court over who is right and who is wrong.

You could be damaging the team and the business without even knowing it.

# Chapter 18
# The immature entrepreneur

W ell done! You've hired one, two or maybe more new staff members. You've built a system, the leads are flowing, the clients are happy and you're feeling good. You're thinking less like a technician and more like an owner.

But there's a little voice in the back of your head whispering, 'Hang on. This doesn't feel right. This is too serene; too peaceful. You're not used to this. You need to throw a few curveballs into the mix to generate that adrenaline that you've come to know and love. You need to shake things up a bit!'

So, you attend a few networking events, read some inspiring business books or watch a couple of TED Talks and come up with some interesting and enterprising ideas you'd like to implement. You waltz into the office, all energised and invigorated and announce, 'Hey team! Listen up. We're doing really well right now, but from now on we're going to do even better! We're going to introduce this new product and change things up a bit so we can flex, scale and grow to the next level. From now on, Sarina, you're going to do this.

Nick, you're going to do that. Rita, you're going to do this and that. And we're all going to start on this new thing right *now*! This is so exciting!'

It may be exciting for you, but I can say with certainty it is not exciting for your team. They find this change of direction very unsettling, mostly unnecessary and utterly annoying. If you're this sort of entrepreneur who sets the team in motion and then changes course without giving notice, you could be damaging the team and the business without even knowing it — and jeopardising everything you've worked for.

There's a reason why entrepreneurs do this. No, it's not self-sabotage, although there's an element of that. It's actually biology.

## The dopamine trap

Entrepreneurs, by their very nature, love the challenge of starting something new; of bringing an idea to fruition. This pursuit of 'the new' gives them a rush of adrenalin, a hit of dopamine. It's a drug, it's addictive and they will do anything to sustain it. That's why they pursue one new initiative after another, before the last one has even had time to get established.

They've succumbed to the 'bright, shiny, object' syndrome, or as I call it, the 'immature entrepreneur's trap'. It afflicts those who lack the emotional intelligence to know how they operate and how their behaviour impacts their team.

This behaviour is acceptable if it affects just you. But it doesn't. You're not a technician any more. You've got a team, and as the leader of the team, you set the tone and the team take their cues from you. So, when you burst into the room with all guns blazing about this new whiz-bang idea or project, and you think everyone is going to be as excited about it as you, you will be sadly mistaken. Sarina, Nick and Rita are quietly thinking, 'I thought we were going in this direction, and now we're not. We've pulled out all stops to get this project up and running, and now you're telling us that we're pursuing a new goal that has nothing to do with what we've been doing for the past three months. Well, that's just great. Terrific.'

They're also thinking, 'What problem are we solving here, because this looks completely different from the problem we were solving yesterday.'

The problem they're solving is that you, the entrepreneur, are bored and need a chemical hit; the problem they're solving is that you need to feel your back up against the wall to generate that addictive rush!

But like the good team members they are, they reluctantly comply with your instructions, put their heads down and get on with bringing your new vision to life. The idea gains momentum, the team get into the groove and they all settle into this new rhythm.

Fast forward three months, and you start to feel scratchy, bored and disinterested again. Maybe it's because sales aren't as strong as you thought they'd be; maybe you received some negative customer feedback, or you lost a major client. Maybe, just maybe, the dopamine high has worn off and you need another shot of adrenaline.

You burst into the office again and say, 'Hey team, look, sorry. That idea we've all been working on for three months? It didn't work. My bad. So, now we're all going to revert to the original strategy: the one I told you to forget about. Okay? Right! Let's get started. This is so exciting!'

Now they are *really* confused, annoyed and frustrated. They've taken the time to learn how to play this new game, and now they're being asked to play yet another game and learn all the new rules that go with it. They start to doubt your capacity to lead and wonder if you've got the ticker to make the business a success. Employees are not entrepreneurs. They think differently from you and want different things from their working life, like stability, certainty and continuity. They can't pivot intellectually as quickly as you. They don't have the need for a dopamine hit.

Your team, exhausted by the constant reversals, says, 'You know what? This is too stressful. I can't cope with the constant change. I didn't sign up for this. I'm out of here.' So they leave, taking all their accumulated knowledge and experience with them.

## Avoiding the immature entrepreneur trap

Does this scenario resonate with you? The reason I'm so familiar with it is because I was that immature entrepreneur. I fell into this trap back when I was 26 and it took me ten years to get out of it and work out what I was doing wrong, and why. I wish I'd known about this syndrome a lot earlier. I could have gone a whole lot further and a whole lot faster if I had.

The good news is this trap is easily avoidable. It starts with being curious and taking time to explore the rationale behind your strategies. For example, when you get excited and want to introduce new products, ideas or innovations, step back for a moment and:

- ask your customers, 'Is this something you want?'
- ask your team, 'Is this something we should do?'
- ask yourself:
  - » What is the exact problem we are solving here?
  - » Is it a goal?
  - » Will this get us closer to our goal?
  - » Is this on my 'to do' list?
  - » Is this where we should be spending time?
  - » How does this fit into our mission?

Print out these questions, pin them on the wall and before you introduce any new strategy or concept, ask yourself these questions. It will prevent you from falling into the immature entrepreneur trap and help you keep your team loyal, steady and strong.

# Staying focused

Studies show that teams need their leader to demonstrate certain emotional states to keep the team on a steady keel. Like a boat in rough waters, without the ballast provided by the leader, the team can feel they are sinking.

The three emotional drivers that makes teams feel safe are:

1.  Safety

    When the leader changes direction without warning, the team asks, 'Do I feel safe? How will this affect my standing in the pecking order of the tribe? Does this new project mean my status is downgraded?'

2.  Surety

    Your team may be asking, 'Does this new project mean my role is now up for grabs? What will happen to all the work I've just done? Will that get used? Will I have to start again?' Certainty is a basic human need. Without it, we feel untethered.

3.  Sovereignty

    New projects and new team formations upset the power dynamic. The team asks, 'Why are we doing this? Who do I report to now? Do I have autonomy over the work I am doing? Do I still have a job?' Your team are not necessarily stoic people. They look to you for guidance and to set the ballast. Without firm answers to these questions, they can feel blindsided and unsafe.

    The cure? Be *aware* of the dopamine trap, *anticipate* its arrival and *resist* the urge to create something new every time you feel bored or restless. Be *curious* about what problem this new initiative will solve, *interrogate* your motive, *stay* the course and *stick* to the plan. The future of your company rests on it.

# The key emotion that kills a partnership is resentment.

# Chapter 19
# Why partnerships don't work

I 've worked with over 10 000 businesses over 18 years and presented to over 50 000 people about how and why businesses fail. If it's a multi-partner venture, the number one reason why the business breaks down is because the partnership blows up.

In the short term, partnerships can work well, but long term? Not so much. So, it will not come as a shock to hear me say, 'I don't like business partnerships.' On average, they don't work. Sure, we see the celebrity partnerships like the AfterPays of the world succeed, but what we don't see are the thousands of partnerships that end up in mediation, arbitration or litigation.

The key emotion that kills a partnership is resentment: One partner feels that they put in more effort, are more focused, and is more set on rapidly growing the business than the other. Or one partner puts in the bulk of the seed funding and thinks that absolves them from doing any of the work.

Here's a scenario I see play out time and time again.

# HOW NOT TO SET UP A PARTNERSHIP

Paul, Riley and Dustin worked for a commercial real estate company. Paul is a qualified builder, Riley is a sales director and Dustin is a chartered accountant. Each harboured a desire to launch their own business, so when all three got retrenched, they thought, 'Now's the time.' They hired a co-working space, got their T-shirts printed and commenced operations.

They won some big tenders, built a small team and paid themselves a decent wage. After 18 months, Paul said, 'I want to take some money out of the business to fund a renovation on my house.'

Riley said, 'I want to take some money out of the business to buy a new car.'

Dustin said, 'I don't want you to take any money out of the business because I'm an accountant, and I don't like spending money unless we have to.'

Paul was not happy with Dustin's decision. He said, 'I've spent the past 18 months working my butt off. I've been on site at 5 am every morning in the freezing cold, pissing in a portable dunny and dealing with psycho subcontractors like Jacko and Jonno. They got arrested last night. They went pig shooting, got caught for speeding and the cops found a stash of hash in the glove box so I had to go down and bail them out, or they wouldn't have been on site this morning to finish the job. I've been through hell, I've earned the right to take some money out of the account and I want that money now.'

Riley wasn't happy with Dustin's decision either. 'I've spent the last 18 months working my butt off too. I've been on the road for six weeks trying to raise capital. My wife hates me, my kids don't know me and I've stacked on seven kilos from eating at Nando's every night. I'm flying cattle class, I've got DVT and the pressure socks are friggin' killing me. I've been through hell and I've earned the right to take some money out of the account and I want that money now.'

Dustin, the accountant, had his own sob story.

'I've been stuck in the office dealing with menopausal Maureen who can't stay awake, and neuro-diverse Nathan who needs constant breaks. Petunia's gone on mat leave, so I had to get a temp. She didn't bother showing up, so the BAS didn't get submitted, which meant I sat on speed dial for three days waiting for the ATO to answer, which they didn't, so we got fined. We've got a recession on the way and if you take money out now it will leave us exposed and we won't be able to make payroll.'

Paul and Riley are unmoved by Dustin's protestations. After a few beers one night, they agreed that Dustin was just a glorified bookkeeper and that any monkey from H&R Block could do what he does. So they decided to cut Dustin loose. Dustin got retrenched, Paul got his reno and Riley got his Renault.

The business continued to grow, do well and make money. 'Getting rid of Dustin was a great idea!' they said to each other. 'We should have done that aaages ago!'

Then the economic conditions changed. Inflation went up and so did interest rates. The cost of raw materials skyrocketed and demand for new builds plummeted. Their COO walked out and took their top three clients with him. A big deal that was meant to be 'a done deal' didn't get done, and the cash flow went into freefall.

Paul, stressed, turned on Riley and said, 'Hey, why haven't you brought any business in? I've got guys sitting around on site with nothing to do. We're bleeding cash. How come we haven't won any work?'

Riley, on the defence, fought back. 'Why did you buy so much stock when you knew we didn't have the work? You've gone over on every job, the profit margins are zero and the overtime you're paying the contractors is killing us. How come you can't control costs?'

They both think the same thing: 'This just isn't working. Why did I get into this caper in the first place? I had a cushy nine-to-five job, a car, phone, expense account, a nice office and four weeks' holiday a year. I've blown my payout on this rubbish and all I've got for it is stress, debt and worry.'

So, they wound up the company and took a job back at their old firm.

That's why partnerships often fade out after only five to seven years. It takes that long for the rot to set in, the cracks to show and the resentments to kick in.

# TOP SIX TIPS FOR BUILDING A STRONG BUSINESS PARTNERSHIP

If you want to start a business partnership, my first piece of advice is, don't. But if you're headstrong and think things will be different for you, and you just can't imagine going it alone, here are my top six tips for how to make that partnership work.

## 1. Have an exit plan

A business partnership is like a marriage. Easy to enter into, hard to get out of. It takes so little to *start* a business that people are lulled into thinking it's easy to actually *build* the business. You have a few beers with a mate at the pub, come up with an idea, pay your ASIC fees and you're off and running! You've barely 'dated' or had an in-depth discussion around values, goals or money: how to resolve conflict, what you'll spend money on, who will do what or how success will be measured. At least with a marriage, you hang out together for a few years, write some vows and spend time mulling over the magnitude of your decision. You *think* about what you're doing before you do it.

Before you commit to a business partnership, you need to think about the exit plan and create a pre-nuptial of sorts as to how you're going to get out of it, before you get into it.

## 2. Write a dis-agreement

Like marriages, most business partnerships start with high hopes and good intentions, so while the goodwill is still good, use that time to write a dis-agreement Yes, a dis-agreement. This document sits to the side of your standard shareholder's agreement and its purpose is to identify in advance every scenario that could trip you up, catch you out or form the foundation of an argument. It's similar to a pre-mortem in that you act *as if* a specific disagreement has already happened, and you create a action plan for how to fix it. If or when the conflict does arise, you have a strategy and can deal with it quickly without a lot of emotional turmoil.

Here are some prompts to help you kick start your dis-agreement checklist:

- What would be the top ten scenarios that would make this partnership untenable and force us to go our separate ways?

- What do we do when we have one of these disagreements? What is the process for resolving it?

- Under what conditions would this agreed process not work?

- What could I do or say (or *not* do or say) that would make you resent me?

- What is our yardstick for success?

- Why would we succeed as a partnership when so many others have failed?

- What are the steps we need to take to dissolve this partnership?

- Who will pay for the dissolution if there is no money in the business bank account?

- Who will be responsible for any debts that are left outstanding?

## 3. Shit test your assumption

When you get married, you commit to a life partner. When you start a business partnership, you commit to a business partner *and their life partner,* and that person often has a thing or two to say about how things run and get done. The partnership can get, as Princess Diana said of her own marriage, 'very crowded' because each person comes to the partnership with a bunch of assumptions, most of them unwarranted, unrealistic and almost certainly unspoken. If those assumptions are not shit tested, teased out or interrogated the partnership is doomed to fail.

## 4. Choose your partner carefully

I get very worried when I see two technicians get together as business partners. It's a guaranteed recipe for failure, unless both have a high degree of emotional awareness and take active steps to minimise conflict.

The best way forward is for one to take on the role of CEO and for the other to stay on as the technician. This is still not ideal as that technician still thinks they have the deciding vote as to how things get done—which they don't—which will cause a raft of other issues.

Ideally, a third party takes on the role of CEO so the technicians can get on with the work they like and do best.

They can also minimise potential for conflict if they do the following:

- Create a formal structure and organisational chart for the business, with clear lines of reporting

- Write clear and precise job descriptions as to who will do what, when and how quickly

- Develop a performance review process to objectively assess the progress of each team member, including the partners

- Establish an advisory board that meets monthly and is independently chaired

- Agree on a third-party mediator to moderate conversations if they can't agree on important decisions

- Schedule regular conversations and have a documented process for discussing concerns, resentments and grievances.

## 5. Have an uncomfortable conversation

What if you're already in a toxic partnership? What if the goodwill has gone and you can't instigate any of these precautionary measures? If that's the unfortunate case, you need to be prepared to have some uncomfortable conversations.

It takes two to tango so for every grievance you have with your partner, they will probably have one with you too. Before you launch into this strategy for dealing with an underperforming partner, display some curiosity into your own actions to ensure you see the whole situation from their perspective.

Here's what to say to a partner who's not pulling their weight or doing what they should be doing:

*Hey, I'm not good at having uncomfortable conversations. I feel really awkward about something that I need to talk to you about. I don't really know how to say it succinctly because I'm just getting used to having these discussions. But in short, I need to let you know that I am starting to resent you, and that the current state of play is not working from my side and I need to have a conversation with you about working through that. Here are the five things I'm concerned about ...*

After you deliver this Oscar-winning speech, you outline your concerns, tell them how you want the situation to be different and detail the actions and behaviours you want to see.

You follow up with:

*For this partnership to be successful, I need you to exhibit these behaviours and carry out these actions. Is that something you can agree to?*

If they say 'no,' then you must work your way through each item of concern, identify what part of it they disagree with and find some form of compromise.

If they still disagree, you need to flag that the relationship cannot work and that you'll need to continue running the business with a dysfunctional partnership (not ideal), or part ways.

## 6. Set the cadence for communication

Resentment festers if it's not dealt with quickly. The longer you leave it, the harder it is to fix, so it pays to nip it in the bud by scheduling regular catchups with your partner.

You can't leave these meetings to chance. They need to be scheduled, diarised and attended. Don't let apathy set in. As time goes on, one or other of the party will want to reduce the cadence of the quarterly.

'We don't need to meet, do we?'

'I'll catch up with you for a coffee next week.'

'Do we need to talk? No? All good.'

This won't cut it. The best way to prevent conflict is to conduct regular, diarised and honest conversations.

I know it's controversial to say that you should not partner with someone to build a business. Every accelerator, incubator and angel investor will tell you the opposite, but I don't see overwhelming success come from forming a business partnership. I see bitterness, regret and resentment.

However, if you are hell bent on building a partnership and you simply can't do it alone, follow these principles and you'll minimise the likelihood of conflict and increase the chances of success. The future of your business depends on it.

# PART III TAKEAWAYS

1. When hiring, choose people who are good at doing the things you like least.

2. Initiate an internship program to train up new staff. It helps eliminate recruitment fees, identifies A-grade players and tests out employees before hiring them.

3. Create an intranet site to house all your induction training materials. It's easy to update, simple to distribute and everyone knows exactly where to find the company's policies and procedures.

4. Identify your corporate values, make them visible and ensure everyone knows what you stand for.

5. Invest in your business book library. For $30 a book you can buy access to the world's great business minds. When you have a problem, turn to the book that provides the solution and apply it.

6. If you have to sack someone, do it quickly, as nicely as you can and take some of the blame for the situation.

7. Don't let underperforming staff get away with delivering poor results or bad behaviour. It tells the rest of the team the standard you are willing to accept.

8. Not all customers are created equal. Focus on the 20 per cent that deliver profits and eliminate the 80 per cent that chew up time, effort and attention and yet deliver little in return.

9. Entrepreneurs can be addicted to the dopamine rush. Stay focused on the task at hand and resist the urge to introduce new initiatives unconnected to your goals.

10. If you can possibly avoid it, don't take on a business partner.

11. If you do take on a partner, write a dis-agreement (the opposite of an agreement) before you go into business together.

12. Have a documented exit plan in case the partnership turns sour.

# PART IV

# MARKETING

Few businesses have the budget to market their business effectively. The good news is you don't need a big budget to make a big impact. One question, asked correctly, will consistently unlock the secrets to understanding exactly what your customers want and empower you to deliver it, with almost zero dollars.

Hands up if you like selling? I thought not. Everyone hates it, but what if you didn't? What if you approached every sales opportunity with excitement and confidence? You can. I've spent two decades perfecting a sales script that works for anyone, no matter what you sell, who you sell it to or what the product is worth.

This 'done for you' script takes the guesswork out of selling, provides the framework for asking the right questions, in the right order at the right time. It's a foolproof, tried and tested system that lets you, or your team, deliver exceptional and exponential results, and will have prospects eating out of your hand and signing that contract within minutes.

If you thought connecting with your industry colleagues and sector is a good thing, think again. Not only can it limit your thinking, it can cost you your business and shut down the prospect of innovation. Sometimes it's wiser to take the path not well travelled. I'll show you why.

Struggling to get motivated? We've all been there. So, what's the secret for overcoming lethargy, lack of energy and overwhelm? It's buried deep in your psyche, but one question can unlock the puzzle that stops you from getting what you want and give you the momentum you need to think big and do what's needed to achieve your big hairy audacious goals.

# Experience always trumps opinion, and execution always trumps planning.

# Chapter 20
# Get some skin in the game

T hey say don't meet your heroes. If you work in accreditation that is certainly true (more on that later). But sometimes meeting your heroes can be life changing. Meeting Gary Vaynerchuk changed mine.

Widely known as Gary Vee, this Belarus-born American entrepreneur took his dad's bricks and mortar wine store and turned it into a $30 million internet behemoth. Gary was also an early investor in Facebook, Uber and Twitter and funnelled those millions into his own enterprises, and is now one of the world's most popular entrepreneurs on social media. Gary says that if you want to build a brick wall you need to put bricks in it.

## Meet Gary Vee! Live in London!

In November 2019 I attended an entrepreneurs' conference in Sydney. It was morning tea time. Everyone had exited the room but I was still in my chair making some notes. An advertisement appeared on the big screen above the stage:

*GVX. The Gary Vee Experience. Get up close and personal in this fully immersive experience! Live in London! Text us now!*

I was interested until I read the 'London' bit. I had heard of Gary, had read about his incredible success stories and was super keen to work with him. The price tag to do so? $100 000. My business was not going well at that time. I was barely making payroll. There was no way I could divert $100 000 to personal development. I parked the idea. *Maybe next year, when we're doing better.*

But the thought of meeting Gary Vee *in person* nagged at me so I sent a text. My motivation was at an all-time low (which is why I attended the conference to start with). I knew that I could be more successful, but I didn't know what to do differently.

The day after the conference finished, I received a phone call from the Gary Vee team.

*Are you in or out? You have 24 hours to make a decision.*

Every fibre of my financial being screamed, *You can't afford to go!* But my instinct—something I try to pay attention to—screamed, *You can't afford not to!*

I woke up the next morning, still thinking about the event. I had to decide. I checked the bank account. Not good. The deadline loomed. It was now or never. What the hell! I slapped down the credit card, paid the fee and booked my ticket. I knew if I didn't put some serious money behind my business endeavour, I would never activate any of it when I got back. I sincerely believe you need to spend money to make money and to hold yourself accountable. I hoped that spending $100 000 on this training would give me the leverage I needed to get moving with my social media campaign.

A month later I was smack bang in the middle of London, sitting in the foyer of The Park Lane Hotel. (That's the blue hotel on the

Monopoly Board, the one next to Mayfair.) It was Christmas time; the hotel was festooned with fairy lights and the street was buzzing. I sat in the foyer waiting for the event to start and watched the dazzling array of sheikhs, celebrities and supermodels make their way in and out of this beautiful hotel.

I expected to see a large gathering at the conference, but it was just me and nine others. Good. That would give me more time with Gary. I thought he was going to teach us about social media and how to leverage it to build your content empire. But he went much deeper.

He talked about the role of entrepreneurs in society, how we have to give back in order to get and how we need to build a legacy. I'd never heard an entrepreneur talk so openly about vulnerability and why it's our duty to help others succeed. His ethos matched mine, but I'd never met anyone who incorporated those values into building multimillion-dollar businesses.

Gary talked at length on a wide range of disparate yet related topics, many of them antithetical to what you'd expect to hear from a self-made multimillionaire:

- *Stop trying to convert your customers:* Don't try to convert the unconvertable

- *Be generous:* Give with no expectation of return

- *Bet on your strengths:* Don't dwell on your weaknesses. Everybody else is already doing that for you

- *Be self-aware:* Figure out who you are, optimise who you are, but never apologise for who you are

- *Take massive action:* When it comes down to it, nothing trumps execution

- *Create content:* You don't decide what's quality. The market does.

A bonus surprise was meeting a raft of Gary's celebrity business collaborators. Some of the most famous business names on the planet popped by to say hello and share their nuggets of wisdom with us.

I met Tom Bilyeu (he runs the Impact Theory YouTube channel, co-founded the protein bar brand Quest Nutrition in 2010 and sold it for a cool $1 billion in 2019).

Ryan Holiday stopped by (Ryan is a college dropout who became the number one *New York Times* bestselling author of legendary books including *The daily stoic, Ego is the enemy* and *Courage is calling*).

Sahar Hashemi came in (she co-founded Coffee Republic, the UK's first US-style coffee bar chain, and sold the business for $200 million).

It was a roll call of the world's most famous corporate identities, and here they were, sitting in front of us, regaling us with their rollercoaster ride of how they built their businesses. It was, as they say in the ads, priceless.

When it was time to leave, I asked Gary to autograph the book he gave me. He wrote just two words:

*Do more.*

It was profound in its simplicity: so profound, in fact, I didn't know what to do more of!

Gary is all about using social media to grow your business. I took his point, but I was a tad dubious. If I was selling sneakers, or wine, or coaching, sure, using social media makes sense. But I was selling audits, accreditation and certification! Hardly the sexiest of services to be showcasing on Insta! I mean, how would you even do that?

So, while I loved learning from Gary and his team, I did leave the event thinking that those marketing strategies might work for others, but they probably wouldn't work for me. Besides, I had already tried using social media to build my accreditation business and it had not worked. But I valued and respected his insights, and felt utterly committed to actioning the tasks he had set me. It would have felt disrespectful towards him to do otherwise.

Before I left London, I shared my reservations with Gary and asked for his advice. This is a precis of how the conversation went. It's not quite word for word, but close to it:

**Kobi:**  Hey Gary, I'm feeling a bit lost with all this social media stuff. Where do I start?

**Gary:**  You need to do more.

**Kobi:**  Of what?

**Gary:**  Everything.

**Kobi:**  Can you be more specific?

**Gary:**  You need to post more.

**Kobi:**  On YouTube?

**Gary:**  On everywhere. Let me ask you, *How often do you post a week?*

**Kobi:**  Twice.

**Gary:**  Kobi, my friend. We have some work to do. By March, that's three months from now, you need to be posting 1000 posts a week.

**Kobi:**  A week?

**Gary:**  A week.

**Kobi:**  But ... but ...

**Gary:**  A week. Kobi, if you want to build a wall, you need to put bricks in the wall. And remember, practice does not make perfect. Only *perfect practice* makes perfect so get going. Stop thinking and start implementing!

I have to be honest. I wasn't convinced this strategy of just creating 1000 posts for the sake of creating 1000 posts would achieve much. Other than LinkedIn, I felt social media wasn't the right vehicle for my type of business. But if that's what Gary says ...

I arrived back in Sydney. I was pleased to see my wife and family, but coming back to the office was a harsh reality check. From the plush confines of The Park Lane Hotel, and glittering dinners with the 'who's who' of entrepreneurship, I now had to face the fact that my business was going very badly. Sales had been sluggish before I left, and had slumped even further while I was gone.

January, a notoriously slow time for our sector, was approaching and the sales pipeline was empty. My credit card bill arrived too, which underlined how much that trip cost and how much I still owed. My logical brain kicked in and the doubts about social media that been dispelled when in Gary's presence, reared their ugly head again. Some of the criticism came from my most trusted advisors:

**My accountant:** Why would you waste time on social media?

**My business coach:** What's the point of posting if you don't have any followers?

**My marketing manager:** Who will write it and post it?

**Me:** What if what I post is crap?

I emailed Gary and shared with him my concerns.

**Kobi:** Gary, I just can't see how all this posting is going to generate leads.

**Gary:** Kobi, this is not about leads. It's naïve to think one post, or even 1000 posts will generate a lead. It's about brand, okay? It's about practising to get better at what you do. It's about showing up in the forums where your customers hang out. It's about dominating the airwaves so that when people need what you offer, the first person they think about is *you*! It's about *brand*! *Brand! Brand!* You got that?

**Kobi:** Yes, Gary.

**Gary:** Now get the fuck on with it and start posting!

**Kobi:** Yes, Gary.

Were it not for the fact I was meeting up with Gary in New York two months from then, I don't know if I would have actually done everything he told me to do.

So, we went to work. It was not easy. We were novices at the social media game. We started with 10 posts, went to 20, doubled it to 40, doubled that, doubled it again and within a few months, we'd reached our goal of posting 1000 pieces of content a week across the top platforms: Instagram, LinkedIn, Twitter and YouTube. The content we created at the start was pretty ordinary, but as we got going and got into the flow, the quality of the content started to improve!

## How to be 300 years ahead of your competitors

We all want a competitive advantage. Posting frequently on social media can give it to you. Think about it. If my competitor posts once a day and I post 100 times a day, by the end of the year, we have practised more than them and technically speaking, are 300 years ahead of them in terms of experience. We all know the adage that we need to train for 10000 hours to master a skill. Social media is no different. If you were a betting person, would you think you'll get a better result with hundreds of posts a day or one post a day? Who is better placed to comment on whether it works or not? You are, because even if it didn't work as you planned, you learned something along the way and can now do it differently—and better.

Experience always trumps opinion, and execution always trumps planning.

## How to 10× your goals

Gary's big on 10×-ing your goals and playing the long game, so I decided to double down on the marketing and host a two-day national conference to generate even more content for our social campaign. We were haemorrhaging cash but I figured since I went all that way to London to be trained by the world's best, I had better put what I had learned into action. We pulled out all stops to put on the most spectacular conference that our customers and suppliers had ever experienced. We hired a stunning venue overlooking Sydney, booked some of the best speakers in Australia, engaged Sydney's society caterers for the food and beverages, and hired a suite of AV and IT experts to create a rip-snorting, tub-thumping motivational event that would have the sector buzzing.

We called the event '2020 Vision', which was ironic because we sure as hell did not see what was coming around the corner.

On 24 March 2020, four weeks after the conference, the then Prime Minister of Australia, Scott Morrison, took to the podium at Parliament House and uttered those fateful words that would literally change the face of this nation: 'COVID-19 is here. Go home. And stay there, until further notice.' Not since the Spanish flu of 1918 has a peacetime government issued such a dire directive, the consequences of which are still being felt, and will continue to be felt, for decades to come.

Like almost everyone in the world, I panicked. I'd been through the 1988 recession, the Gulf War, the Y2K Millennium Bug debacle, the 2008 Global Financial Crisis and more. But this was new, and very, very different. We were in uncharted waters. I'd heard many sociologists say that the 'veneer' that connects a civilised society is thinner than we think and when people feel threatened, it doesn't take much to turn them against each other. And they were right.

Fights over toilet paper and pasta broke out in suburban supermarkets.

People dobbed on their neighbour for going outside or not wearing a mask.

Police arrested law-abiding citizens for posting on Facebook from the privacy of their own home.

Was this the end of civilisation as we knew it? The panic was palpable. The fear was real.

## The day the world changed

I'd like to pretend I was stoic and strong during those early days of COVID-19, but I was worried. Desperately worried. Unfortunately for us, our business does not meet a basic human need; we don't make hand sanitiser or sourdough. We do audits! Who needs a safety manual for how to handle a fire extinguisher if there's no one in the building! Who needs a business audit when there's no business to audit! While we were already cloud based and totally geared up to work remotely, our clients weren't. Most didn't even have a web cam! The world froze, our clients froze and our source of leads and paid work froze too.

Some businesses were smashing it. Woolworths did the equivalent of Christmas Eve trading *every day* for 18 months. Kogan, Harvey Norman and JB Hi-Fi were all on fire. Their sales doubled—tripled— practically overnight. For some sectors, it was insane. For others, like mine, it was a cemetery.

I sent everyone home, as instructed. The office was empty. The streets were empty. The shops were empty. It was truly apocalyptic. My first reaction was to put a hold on everything: to pull our advertising, place staff on furlough and cancel the contractors. For the financial security of my family I needed to do what was necessary to ride out this storm and protect what I had.

I figured, if I could just make myself a small target, I could come out the other side, set up shop again as a sole trader and stay afloat that way. After all, no-one knew how long this crisis would last and what would happen next. I had been a sole trader once. Maybe I could do that again?

But this 'thinking small' attitude didn't sit well with me. It never has. I've always been a risk taker, in business and in life. I love taking it to the edge, be it sailing, skiing or hiking. Boundaries are there to be pushed. I also had the voice of Gary Vee ringing in my head.

*Hustle!*

*You can't be heard if you're not communicating!*

*If you don't tell the world what you're doing, who will?*

*Keep posting!*

*Do more!*

I was conflicted. It's one thing to intellectually know what to do. It's another thing to physically act on it. My heart said, *Think big!*, but my head said, *Stay small!* It was a confusing time. How could I take back control over my destiny?

When in doubt, I always go back to basics and keep the question simple. The question I asked myself was this:

*Kobi, if you were a gambling man and you were placing a bet, where would you place your money? On the guy doing more marketing, or less marketing?*

It was a no-brainer. I'd bet on the guy doing more marketing. It's what Gary would do too.

## Listen to your instinct

In the words of entrepreneur and speaker Hans F Hansen, 'It takes nothing to join the crowd. It takes everything to stand alone.' When you're under stress, it's tempting to follow others, abdicate decision making and run with the crowd. But at some point, you have to pay attention to your own instinct—to listen to the little voice inside you and do what you need to do. On the few occasions when I have not listened to my instinct, it has cost me a great deal.

When I first launched Simmat and Associates in 2004, I built a very simple website to help promote it. The website was built using Dreamweaver software (remember that?), so it actually wasn't that simple, but it was sufficient.

We were just starting out, business was slow and we needed this website up to help us get some runs on the board. I said to my marketing manager at the time, Suzy, a lady I deeply respected, 'Let's run a pay per click [PPC] campaign, drive some traffic to the website and drum up some business.'

She looked at me and said, 'Kobi, that is not a good idea. Money is already tight and driving paid traffic to a substandard website will do us more harm than good.'

'But any traffic is better than no traffic,' I said.

'No, it's not,' she said. 'That is not a good use of our limited marketing budget. It will damage our brand.'

I reluctantly accepted her advice without protest.

This may come as a surprise to many, but back then—and even now sometimes—I struggled with impostor syndrome. This condition manifests in all sorts of unhelpful ways: I think other people know better than me, or that they know something I don't. I fail to back myself or put my opinions forward.

I am a self-made, self-taught business owner so I don't always have a lot of theoretical knowledge to back up my instinctual inclinations. As a result, I am easily led by those I perceive to have more experience. On this occasion, I valued Suzy's experience over my instinct so I took her advice and we put a kibosh on the PPC campaign.

At the time, I could have bought top keywords such as 'accreditation', or 'certification', or 'ISO 9001' for around 5 cents a click. To give you some comparison, those words now cost around $8 a click. Even if we had sent paid traffic to a poor site, it would have been better than nothing, and it would have cost us next to nothing.

My instinct had told me this PPC caper was going to be a game changer, yet I failed to acknowledge it. If I had backed myself, and continued with the PPC campaign, I could have dominated those phrases and I would have gotten to where I am today 10 years faster and for half the cost. It was a poor decision to not pursue that campaign, and one I greatly regret.

Listen to your instinct.

So, I stayed calm, resisted the urge to panic, took the long-game approach, listened to the 'Gary' voice in my head (and my own instinct) and went for it.

We didn't cancel anything or reduce our spending. In fact, we doubled, sometimes tripled it! We sent more emails, wrote more blogs, recorded more videos, made more phone calls. We held Zoom calls for suppliers, ran information sessions for our clients, held group coaching clinics for our staff, launched a new podcast and increased our magazine from 25 pages to 100 pages.

This frenzy of activity went on for months. My staff were at home with nothing to do, so I enlisted their help in creating this flood of content. We were tapping out at well over 1000 posts a week. Gary would have been proud of me.

And then something really weird happened. I checked the price of our critical keywords on PPC. The price had fallen by 90 per cent. I checked the price of placing a pre-roll advertisement on YouTube. It had fallen by 70 per cent. The print advertising fees in leading journals fell by 50 per cent. All the prices were dropping, and not by a little, but by a lot. 'Unprecedented' was probably the most overused word during this time, but this time it was true. These price drops were unprecedented.

I realised very quickly why the prices had dropped. Everyone had stopped advertising and posting, which meant we had no competitors. They'd all packed up and gone home, leaving little ol' me to scoop up the remnants. Whoo hoo! I couldn't believe what was happening. But that little devil on my shoulder piped up again:

*Hey Kobi, are you sure this is the right thing to do?*

*If everyone else is cancelling their marketing, maybe you should too?*

*What if they're right, and you're wrong?*

*Money is already tight. Can you afford to take this risk?*

The memory of going against my instinct flared up. I did not want to repeat the errors from the past. And then Gary's voice piped up again.

*Do more.*

I decided to back myself on this one. I was tired of deferring to others. I was tired of questioning and doubting myself. To be honest, I was just tired full stop. But I knew in my heart of hearts, this was the right thing to do. I gathered the team on Zoom, told them of my decision and I said, 'Hold tight everyone. This is our chance to make a dent. Don't just keep doing what you're doing. Don't even double it. Triple it! Bums down, heads up and let's go!'

The team went into action, creating more content than ever before.

I was so excited. I knew this was the right decision. I woke up each morning, stoked to think of the leads that we'd create overnight. After all, if we were spending all this money, and creating all this content, and no-one was advertising except us, it had to show up in the pipeline, right?

Except it didn't.

I checked, and rechecked, the analytics every day to see where the traffic was coming from, to see what keywords were being clicked, to check what videos were converting, but there was not one uptick in any of the channels. There was no movement at all.

I monitored the dashboard that tracked the incoming phone calls, the outgoing proposals, the leads in the pipeline. Nothing. The sounds of crickets chirping was deafening.

I kept checking, day by day, hour on the hour, but it was the same each time. It was like the channels were frozen.

I felt physically sick. My chest ached with anxiety. I had bet the farm on this one. I had backed myself. I had made this executive decision to double down on this content fiesta and zig when everyone had zagged. I had invested tens of thousands in this strategy and even hired a team of new contractors to help out. My cash flow was haemorrhaging. I still had all the usual overheads of an office: payroll tax, car leases, computers, licence fees, but with no sales! I had listened to my instinct and it had led me astray. I had made a mistake. A big one.

I was exhausted. I had done everything I could have possibly done to turn things around, to honour Gary's advice and activate our social media content empire, but it just hadn't worked. I contemplated how I was going to lay everyone off, cancel their contracts and say my goodbyes. I rehearsed the speech I'd need to give. I knew the time had come. We had done our best and it just hadn't worked.

And then, all of a sudden, my phone started to ring. And then my sales manager's phone started to ring. And then the 1300 number that we'd set up to take advantage of all this 'new business' started to ring, and ring, and ring. And it just kept on ringing. It was like someone had flicked a switch or turned on a tap. We were inundated. Existing clients wanted new proposals. New clients wanted training. Clients of clients wanted accreditation. The demand for coaching went through the roof. Whatever we had, they wanted. It was insane. The phone wasn't the only device ringing and bringing in new business. The website tripled its traffic overnight. My LinkedIn page went from 1400 to 10000 followers in a week. My Instagram account exploded from 1200 to 15000 in two weeks. And the money started to flow. For the first time ever, our bank balance topped $1 million. We struggled to keep up. It was like a river of cash floating into our coffers. I couldn't believe my eyes.

# What happened?

When my team and I finally had the headspace to sit down and reflect on what happened, we realised why the switch had been flicked.

When COVID-19 hit, people were frozen with fear and freaked out at having to work from home, school their kids at the kitchen table and in some states, stay indoors or risk getting arrested.

But once people transitioned to working from home (which happened remarkably quickly), they found that a few things had changed.

First, they discovered they no longer had to spend two hours in a car commuting to work every day, so they had an extra couple of hours up their sleeve to doodle around on Google and see what was going on in their industry. When people needed motivation, education and the tools for implementation, we were there, online, front and centre, and ready to go.

Second, they used that newfound time to continue their professional development (so they could stay relevant in case they lost their job). This caused the consumption of our videos, podcasts and webinars to soar.

Third, the organic traffic to our site exploded, which meant Google placed us in the top position on the search engine results page. This generated more clicks, which meant more of our content was consumed, which meant more 'time on site', which meant Google rewarded us with even more SEO (search engine optimisation) 'juice'. It was a virtuous cycle that kept on giving.

We were one of the few to keep advertising at the time, so we had a monopoly on those idle eyeballs and that translated to a huge surge in interest, awareness and lead generation. While others were cutting back on what they considered 'discretionary' items—such as marketing and advertising—we were ramping everything up and it was paying off in spades.

To cap it off, our team were also working from home, and super motivated to justify their roles and keep the business alive, so they were hyper productive and highly engaged in helping me launch this massive onslaught of online activity and the groundswell of sales that came with it.

By the end of 2020, a mere nine months later, the world was still in a state of shock and so were we, but for a host of different reasons—and all the right ones. We'd well and truly reached our goal of creating 1000 posts a week, we'd filled the pipeline with enough leads to last us a year, our systems were firing on all cylinders and we were making more money than ever before.

We couldn't have known this, but our timing was perfect. We acted quickly, took a leap of faith and were in the right place at the right time. You could say we were lucky. I say we just took massive action in the face of great uncertainty. And it paid off.

# TOP FIVE THINGS YOU NEED TO KNOW ABOUT SOCIAL MEDIA MARKETING

## 1. Don't get hung up on quality

Don't judge the quality of your work. Just create it, post it and let the market determine what's quality content and what's not. You are not the audience and what you like may not be what your clients like. If you can't write to save your life, hire a professional copywriter, or use a speech-to-text app. Just make content.

## 2. Test your content in organic, boost it in paid

Track the organic content that's getting engagement and then use that content in your paid advertising. Why waste money boosting content that's not performing? Take the time to work out which content people love, commit to making more of that, use that in your socials and spend your money on boosting the best-performing content.

### 3. Don't worry about the metrics

Don't not post because you don't have any followers. Take advantage of having zero traction to test new content, play around with different formats and start working out what works. You don't want to be testing new content when you have millions of followers watching your every move.

### 4. Don't expect one post to generate leads

Only 3 per cent of your market is in the market for your service at any one time, which means 97 per cent of people are not in the market for your service most of the time. This means you need to be flying your flag high at all times, turning up in people's feeds and trumpeting your brand as often as you can. Use your socials to build your brand and the leads will follow.

### 5. Have faith

Remember the phrase 'Build it and they will come', from the Kevin Costner film *Field of dreams*? It's the same with social. Post it and they will come. Have faith that what you do will get seen. But you have to post it first. When that 3 per cent of the market does turn up, guess who they'll see? You, that's who. And as we know, it's not what you know, it's not even who you know. It's *who* knows *you*.

Prior to this Gary Vee experiment, we were posting a maximum of two pieces a week. Now we were posting well over 1000 posts every week. The result? Our metrics went through the roof. Sure, they were vanity metrics. But when someone looked me up to invite me onto a podcast, and they saw I had 200000 followers on Instagram, or a publisher checked out my profile to see if I had enough followers to justify a publishing deal, then these numbers mattered a lot. Sales, by the way, soared off the back of all this, and our pipeline was constantly full too.

# How to get started with social media when you don't know what to do

A quick and easy way to kick start your social media journey is to write down the top 20 questions your clients have about your service. For example, in my world the most frequently asked questions are:

- What does a business coach do?

- How much do they charge?

- How often do we meet?

- What process do they use?

- What if I don't get the results I am looking for?

You then answer those questions in a video, put it on your website, on YouTube, Facebook, LinkedIn and Instagram, or send it out as part of an email newsletter.

People in the market for your services are going to be Googling for that content, so give them the answers they need to make a purchasing decision. Whoever can answer those questions will be rewarded well. Google will give you a boost because you're being 'trustworthy and relevant', and the customer will like you for the same reasons.

As Gary Vee says, 'Do more'.

# Envision it, create it and deliver it.

# Chapter 21
# The little club that could

T he Royal Motor Yacht Club of NSW is one of Sydney's finest boating clubs. It's situated on the Hawkesbury River, arguably one of the most spectacular waterways in the world, and offers expansive views, multiple dining areas, a cocktail bar, a wedding venue, an outdoor BBQ area, a balcony and a heated pool. It hosts black-tie gala events, attracts celebrities from around the world and stages world-class regattas. Anyone and everyone with a boat wants to be a member of this club.

And then there's the Kuring-Gai Motor Yacht Club. It's also a yacht club with a fancy title, but unfortunately it does not have the glittering location, membership base or cachet of its nearby competitor. The clubhouse is 'historic', which means it's old, has limited moorings, and, being nestled deep in the heart of a national park, down a very long and steep road, is very difficult to access.

At one point, it was on the point of closure as it just could not survive with the limited support it was receiving.

But the locals didn't want it to die, so they got together and brainstormed ways to stay competitive. They knew they could not go head to head with their glamorous counterpart up the coast, so they asked the questions, 'What can we do well that the other club can't? What can we do differently? What's our unique selling proposition?'

They knew their existing members were mostly families with young children so they decided to eschew being 'all things to all people' and became a 'family-focused' yacht club, vowing to be the best they could be at that. So, they asked the question: 'If we are going to be the "best" family yacht club in the district, *what would a five-star version of that situation look like?*'

This one question unleashed a torrent of ideas and strategies, which resulted in the committee initiating a range of new endeavours. They:

- offered an affordable 'family' rate so that every member of the family could join
- built a playground to accommodate a range of ages
- upgraded their BBQ facilities and created a members' lounge
- added outdoor amenities to make it functional all year round
- held pontoon parties and Sunday night 'happy hour' drinks to encourage socialising and help new members meet others
- held open days to attract new families to the sport
- offered kayak races and 'fishing days' for kids and their parents.

Those initiatives worked and the club soon became the 'go to' club for families. You could say it got a 'second wind'. It is now firing on all cylinders, membership is at capacity and it has never been more profitable.

Many of the members told us later that while they could have easily afforded the more expensive membership fees of the other exclusive club, they preferred the warm, inclusive and informal atmosphere of this little club that could.

The club's membership team discovered that they didn't need to be a five-star operator or charge five-star prices to offer a five-star experience. All they needed to do was commit to serve their members as best they could with the resources they had. It all started with asking the question, *What would a five-star version of this situation look like?*

Envision it, create it and deliver it.

## A five-star dining experience

I have Dan McKinnon to thank for teaching me this principle. When he took me on as a waiter at his upmarket Cottage Point Inn restaurant, he showed me what five-star service looks like and how a simple question could make a massive difference. It was life changing. I now bring that attitude (and that question) to all my interactions with staff, my suppliers and of course, my clients.

Irrespective of how much you charge, you can still think and act like a five-star operator.

Take McDonald's. They own the market for 'fast food at low prices' but they consistently offer a five-star experience every time. Most people don't associate McDonald's with being a five-star dining establishment, but when you buy a burger from them you know the experience is going to be consistently five-star in the sense that:

- the food will be hot, fresh and exactly the same each time
- you will be served with a smile by well-groomed staff
- if the order is wrong, cold or you've just changed your mind, they will refund your money, and do so without a fuss
- there won't be a stray hair in your hamburger or a fingernail in your fries.

McDonald's is a one-star dining establishment in terms of price and atmosphere, but their consistency and dedication to turning a fast-food encounter into a five-star situation creates customer loyalty.

You may be thinking, 'But Kobi, that's all well and good for McDonald's. They're a $154 billion company, with thousands of staff and millions of customers. They can afford to offer a five-star experience. I'm not McDonald's.' But here's the thing. You don't need to be a McDonald's to offer a five-star service and you don't need a big team or budget to deliver on it.

## Compare the pair

I took a taxi to the airport a while back. The driver was late, he got lost getting to the airport, the car reeked of fried food and he talked on the phone the whole way there.

Compare that with the Uber I took from the airport when I returned home. The driver did everything right. He:

- texted me to let me know he had arrived
- got out of the car and opened the door for me
- offered to turn the radio off, up, down or to my preferred station
- asked me if the temperature was to my liking and if I'd like more heat or less
- didn't engage in conversation until I initiated it
- offered me a small bottle of water, mints and a fresh mask.

This driver had clearly come from the Dan McKinnon School of Customer Service, and knew how to turn a basic cab ride into a five-star experience. He understood what it was to be 'of service' and had asked the question, *What would a five-star version of this situation look like?* It cost him very little to create it. Other than the mints, mask and mini-bottle of water, all of those five-star offerings cost him zero.

Of course, I gave him a five-star rating, a generous tip and took his personal business card to book him directly the next time I needed a cab.

# If you don't know what a five-star service looks like, just ask

When I travel, the Hyatt is my hotel of choice. On a recent trip, I checked in at reception at around 3 pm. After much tapping on the computer screen and a couple of phone calls, the man on duty, Taj, said to me:

'I'm very sorry sir. Your room is not ready yet. It is still being prepared. We are very short staffed at the moment.'

'No problem,' I said.

'May I offer you a cup of coffee, a newspaper and a glass of iced water?'

'Thank you, that would be great.' I sat down, he brought it all over, I checked some emails and relaxed.

Thirty minutes later, Taj came back.

'Sir, my sincere apologies for keeping you waiting. The room is still not ready. May I offer you a glass of wine while you wait?'

'Sure, why not?'

At 4 pm, Taj made his way over again.

'Sir, your room is now ready. I will take you up personally.'

He showed me to my room, told me how everything worked and as he left, he said, 'I am very sorry for the delay in preparing your room, sir. Is there anything I can do to make up for the inconvenience you've experienced today?'

'Nothing really,' I said. 'I'm just happy that the room is ready.'

'May I offer you a complimentary breakfast tomorrow morning in our restaurant?'

'Sure, why not?'

'I will take care of it,' he said and departed.

When the inevitable 'we appreciate your feedback' survey popped up in my email, I reflected on my 'check-in' experience.

Was I annoyed at having to wait for the room? A little bit.

Should the room have been ready? Yes.

Should this happen at a five-star hotel? Probably not.

I gave Taj and the hotel a five-star review not because of what happened, but because of how Taj handled it. He:

- owned the problem: 'I'm sorry that the room is not ready'
- gave me a reason: 'We are very short staffed at the moment'
- gave me special attention (a coffee, newspaper, water and wine)
- kept me updated along the way (even when the news was not good)
- asked me how I would like to be compensated for the inconvenience
- gave me a complimentary meal even when it was not asked for.

We live in uncertain and unpredictable times so we have to be flexible and hope that when circumstances conspire against us, our customers cut us some slack too. A five-star operator can't get it right all the time, but it's the way they manage it that makes them a five-star operator.

## Don't worry. They won't want it for free

I used to hold back from asking questions because I honestly thought the client would say 'The five-star version of this situation is that you give me this service for *free*!' Few of us could sustain that offer. But I've discovered that clients rarely, if ever, want something for nothing; they just want to get what it says 'on the box', and if that can't be delivered, they want some recognition of that.

Train your staff to ask the customer questions about what they want and what they like or don't like. Consider what the five-star version of the situation might look like at every stage of the customer journey, especially if or when things get heated. You'll quickly resolve the situation and learn a thing or two about what the customer *really* wants.

Be careful to not let the so-called 'legends' of your industry intimidate, gag or threaten you.

# Chapter 22

# Beware of the Brown Cardigans

When I was 29 and starting out in the audit and accreditation sector, I was ambitious, hungry to learn and eager to meet the legends of the industry. I attended all the conferences, read the books and turned up to all the association events. I wish I hadn't. I thought I would come away inspired, uplifted and motivated. I came away demoralised.

These 'giants' of the industry—men I had looked up to, read about and seen on stage—were nothing like I imagined. They were small-minded, big-bellied buffoons, uniformly attired in beige chinos and fawn sports jackets with patches of leather at the elbow. (Some of them even wore socks and sandals.)

These Brown Cardigans, as I called them, would stand around at their industry conference, a blueberry muffin in one hand, a coffee in the other, flicking the crumbs off their shirts while whingeing to whoever would listen about the state of 'the industry'. Their grievances were around how little the government did to help the sector along, and why the authorities should make the various codes mandatory. When a new innovation emerged, they whinged about that too because it meant they now had to work harder to win the contract.

I really set the cat among the pigeons when I introduced 'fixed price' accreditation contracts. The Brown Cardigan–style pricing strategy was to submit a low-ball quote, get the job and start work. Once the job was underway, the price mysteriously increased due to an 'unforeseen' event. The client, already knee deep in the project and unable to ascertain fact from fiction, had no option but to agree to the variation, pay the increased price and suck it up. The Brown Cardigan would rub his fat, sweaty hands with glee, pocket the profit and move onto the next unsuspecting victim. This was an industry-wide, and accepted, practice.

I was appalled at the deception and found the process totally deplorable. It was unfair, unethical and unsustainable, and I didn't want to operate that way. I talked to a few of my clients and asked them, 'If I could offer you a five-star version of this service, what would it look like?'

'We want a fixed price service' was the unanimous answer. So, that's what I offered: a service that solved their problem, not mine, and every single one of my clients signed up to the service. They wanted it because it met their needs on multiple levels: it gave them cost-certainty that the price would not vary, no matter what. That was a big deal for them. It smoothed out their cash flow, so instead of getting a $12 000 invoice every year, they got a $1000 invoice every month. This meant they could approve the invoice instantly without seeking a senior manager's input, which enabled the job to commence without delay.

In short, the fixed price format was a winner. It was quick to set up and administer, gave them a guaranteed outcome and was cheaper than what they had been paying.

This fixed price format helped me in four critical ways. It:

- provided a regular and reliable cash flow
- gave me a chance to build the relationship with the client and to offer them new and interesting services
- was fast, good and cheap(er) to deliver, which made it easier to sell to them.

In fact, when I was selling my business, all of the prospective buyers told me that this subscription-based model was one of the primary factors that attracted them. Buyers *love* recurring revenue.

This fixed price, subscription-based innovation revolutionised the industry. Everyone loved it. It was honest, ethical and added great value to their business. It was a game changer, for everyone. The only people who didn't love it were the Brown Cardigans. You can imagine what they were saying:

*That little upstart.*

*How dare he come in here and upset the apple cart.*

*We had a good thing going and now look what he's gone and done.*

As far as I was concerned, this was a disruption that had to happen. I was unrepentant. The Brown Cardigans had had it too good for too long. Those dinosaurs could no longer coast along, dragging their knuckles, over-charging and under-delivering. They could no longer pull the wool over the clients' eyes and hope the deception wouldn't be noticed. From now on, they'd have to fight hard to get a client, be transparent with pricing and put the needs of the client above theirs.

To this day, unless absolutely necessary, I don't attend industry functions. I don't go because I don't want to be influenced by the Brown Cardigans, their blinkered approach to business and their limiting beliefs about business.

I don't go because I'm busy. I don't have time to sit around bemoaning the state of the industry. (Have you noticed that attendance at industry events tends to be in inverse proportion to the amount of work the attendees have on?) Ergo, I don't go.

I also don't go because I talk too much and I'm likely to blurt out a new innovation that I am incubating and give away my competitive edge. (I'm a natural sharer and if someone asks for my help or opinion, I'll give it to them, and probably give away my intellectual property while I'm at it.)

'But what about your contribution to the industry, Kobi?' they say. 'Surely you have an obligation to support the sector that supports you? Isn't it your duty to mentor the young guns coming up the ranks?'

Well, yes and no.

My contribution to the industry is to be innovative, to find new and useful ways of being of service to the client; to help the client do their job and deliver a five-star service at the best price.

My obligation to the sector is to raise the standard of service, to inspire everyone around me to be better and to keep progressing.

My duty to the up and coming is to train them to put the customer first, challenge them to dream big and coach them to think for themselves.

Do I care what 'the industry' thinks of me? Not really, because there is no 'industry'. The 'industry' I came into in 2004 was a rag-tag collection of dinosaurs who got together to eat muffins, drink coffee and exchange war stories about how bad the sector had become, and how deficient the government was at helping them fleece their customers. Why would I want to be a part of that?

Clearly, not all industry associations are as moribund as mine. Most offer a helpful, affordable and collegiate source of resources and support for their members. But if you are new to your sector, be careful to not let the so-called legends of your 'industry' intimidate, gag or threaten you. If they try to, just ignore them, because when they say, 'Stop doing what you're doing: you're ruining our industry', what they're really saying is, 'Stop doing what you're doing: you're ruining my nice little scam.'

You need to back yourself, believe in your product, have faith and start selling.

# Chapter 23

# How to sell anything to anyone

I 've coached thousands of business owners. I've seen why some succeed and why many fail. The successful operators have one thing in common: they can sell. It really is as simple as that.

Your ability to build a business is almost entirely predicated on your ability, willingness and capacity to sell your product, service, story and vision to everyone in your ecosystem: your staff, your suppliers and of course, your clients. If you can't do that, you will struggle to succeed.

## Why are people so afraid to sell?

There are a host of reasons why some people don't like selling, but it's mostly because they don't believe in themselves, their product and the value their product offers. If they did, they wouldn't hesitate to sell it. Most people don't like being seen as pushy, insincere or inauthentic. I get it. But let's say you happen to sell bottles of water and you stumble across a man dying of thirst in the desert. Would you feel pushy selling him a bottle of water? No. You'd have no hesitation because it will save that man's life. We can't all sell life-saving services, but we have to act as if we do, or we will buckle at the first sign of buyer resistance.

I know start-up founders are encouraged to find investors as quickly as possible. They're told, 'Why back yourself with your own money when you can persuade some schmuck to fund your wild and crazy experiment?' This strategy just kicks the can down the road for when you eventually have to sell something to someone.

The irony is, many start-ups would rather sell their vision (and their soul, in some ways) to an investor to secure seed funding, than put themselves on the line and sell their product to a customer to fund their expansion. The exception to this is when you're selling complex software or hardware that cannot be built without high levels of technical expertise and many years of software development. My advice? Start selling today, quickly. Fund your own business. Pre-sell your products to customers and see if what you offer will fly. Crowdfund your concept by asking people to pre-order. The best test of a new business idea is, 'Will someone buy it?' If you get even one paying customer, you've got yourself a business. If you start talking about your product, and people say, 'Shut up and take my money!' you are onto a winner. If no-one is interested, you'll need to rethink your plan.

If you want to build a business others want to buy, you need to back yourself, believe in your product, have faith and start selling—now!

# TOP THREE COMMANDMENTS OF AN ETHICAL SALESPERSON

I am an ethical salesperson. This may sound like an oxymoron, but I am in business for the long haul and know that I make more money on future sales than I do on the first. I value my name, my heritage and my reputation. I am not about the quick buck. I'm about creating value for everyone. As such, I like to leave money on the table for everyone in the deal including—and especially—my suppliers. If I don't, they can't sustain a profitable business, and that's not good for anyone.

These are my three commandments for being an ethical salesperson.

## 1. Don't give customers what they want. Give them what they need

It's a universal sales truth that most people don't know what they want, so our job as ethical salespeople is to find out what they really need, and give them that. They may not even know what problem they're solving or what's needed to fix it. You do, so don't hesitate to be upfront about what you think they need.

## 2. Be efficient but don't rush

Give your prospects the gift of time, that most precious of commodities. Take the time to canvass their situation and their objections. If you can't give them the time they need, postpone the sales call until you can. Novice salespeople tend to 'show up and throw up'—they turn up, take over the conversation, dump the features on the prospect and hope something sticks. Crudely known as 'premature elaboration', this approach doesn't work and doesn't save time. It is a waste of time.

### 3. Let them go

If you can't genuinely help someone and believe that what you offer can make a material difference in their life, you are ethically obliged to say 'I can't help you, but I will refer you to someone who can.' They'll appreciate the honesty and the karmic circle will kick in and reward you in some other way, at some other time. Whatever your beliefs, aim to help others even if there's nothing in it for you. As the great boxer Muhammad Ali said, 'Service to others is the rent you pay for your room here on earth.'

# The mistakes novices make when selling

I am not being immodest when I say that I can sell almost anything to anyone. I don't believe there's anything I *can't* sell. Having delivered and witnessed thousands of sales presentations, I've discovered the recipe for creating a kick-arse sales pitch. I've seen a few rookie errors people make that stop them from succeeding.

Following are the biggest mistakes novices make that stop them from selling as much as they could, or should. They:

- stumble around in small talk for too long
- speak too soon, too much and too often
- don't ask enough questions
- don't ask the right questions at the right time
- fail to mention price early enough
- don't establish value
- don't qualify the customer early enough
- don't check liquidity early enough
- wait too long to ask for the sale.

# From cold to sold

No matter what you sell, or who you sell it to, the sales process is the same, give or take a few tweaks. I have a very no-nonsense approach to sales. I teach this process to my team, which has enabled us to generate $50 million in revenue in under two decades.

I've developed a script that helps you navigate the process and handle almost any objection. I call it the SMASH sales process.

# The SMASH sales process

There are five steps to creating a compelling sales pitch. Follow these five steps and you'll get a great result every time. (Keep in mind that sometimes a great result is getting a quick 'no' so that you can cut ties quickly and move onto servicing other higher quality prospects. Time is money.)

These are the five SMASH steps:

1. Set up the sales conversation
2. Massive information gathering
3. Acknowledge their responses
4. Showcase the service
5. Handle objections.

'What about closing the sale?' you ask. 'Shouldn't that be the last step in the process?' No. Don't leave the 'close' to the end. You should follow the ABC of sales: Always Be Closing (more on this shortly).

Let's now put the SMASH sales process to the test with a mythical client called Brenda Brown. I use the SMASH sales process every day when I'm selling my coaching services to people like Brenda.

This is Brenda's background:

*Client:* Brenda Brown

*Age:* 43

*Business:* Commercial cleaning

*Turnover:* $500 000 per year

*Staff:* 4

*Location:* Brisbane.

Here's Brenda's problem:

Brenda runs a commercial cleaning business. She's 'on the tools' most nights cleaning multistorey office towers in downtown Brisbane. Her goal is to move away from being the 'technician' (i.e. doing the work) and create a systematic, turnkey business that she can sell.

Brenda wants to hire a business coach to help her achieve her goal. She's worked with some coaches in the past but has never had success. She is unsure if my coaching service will benefit her business and is cautious about committing.

Here's how I employ the five-step SMASH process to handle prospects like Brenda.

## 1. Set up the sales conversation

You need to qualify prospects quickly. Don't stuff around with too much small talk. Just jump in. There are four elements to the set-up. The four elements make up the KICS process:

- Kick off the conversation and elicit their goals
- Introduce the product, price and outcome
- Check liquidity
- Seal the deal with a soft close.

Here's the script to use to conduct your sales conversations.

# IDEAL SALES CONVERSATION SCRIPT

**Kobi:** Hey Brenda, it's great to be chatting.

In thinking about a year from now, what does success look like?

*Kick off the conversation—but not for too long. Get to the point.*

*(You can't sell anything if you don't know what they want. Resist the temptation to talk about your product or service at this stage of the process. It's too early. You have one mouth and two ears and they should be used in this proportion.)*

*Elicit their goals.*

**Brenda:** I'd like to double my annual revenue from $500 000 to $1 million.

**Kobi:** Right. Sounds good. I believe that my coaching process can help you achieve that goal or accelerate it.

I charge $5000 a month for my services, and what you're going to get for that fee is full access to me and my team, and an absolute guarantee that you will achieve your goal of at least doubling your revenue— and you're going to reach that goal in 18 months.

Is that something you would like to achieve?

*Introduce the product, price and benefit.*

*Establish the price and the value of your service (i.e. what they get) quickly.*

*Check in to get a 'yes'.*

*(You need around seven small 'yeses' to get to the big 'yes'—i.e. the sale.)*

**Brenda:** Wow. That sounds amazing.

| Kobi: | Cool. Let me ask: Are you liquid for $5000 per month? |
|---|---|
| | *Check their liquidity to see if they can afford you.* |
| | *(There is no point continuing the conversation if they can't afford you. A prospect is always assessing two elements: value and affordability.)* |
| Brenda: | Yes, I am. |
| Kobi: | Great. So, when would you like to start? |
| | *Seal the deal with a soft close.* |
| Brenda: | Today? |
| Kobi: | Terrific. I'll get your direct debit form sent over right now. |
| | *Seal the deal with a soft close.* |

*We wish …!*

If only it was that easy, right? No objections, no questions, instant success. Sometimes the sales process *can* be as quick and simple as this. But what if Brenda can't afford my services? Let's replay the process and see what happens.

## ALTERNATIVE SALES CONVERSATION SCRIPT (I)

| Kobi: | Cool. Let me ask: Are you liquid for $5000 per month? |
|---|---|
| | *Check their liquidity to see if they can afford you.* |
| Brenda: | No, I'm not unfortunately. |
| Kobi: | Awesome. Can I ask, is it because you can't afford $5000 per month or you just don't see the value? |
| | *Check to see if their resistance is due to affordability or value. If it's affordability…* |

> **Brenda:** I really can't afford the $5000 per month.
>
> *Outline payment plans and other strategies for making the $5000 palatable.*
>
> **Kobi:** Right. Okay, no problem. You are most welcome to check out all my free resources on my website. There's a host of content there that you'll find valuable.
>
> *Move her on to your database, send her your email newsletter and keep her as a warm prospect.*

Let's replay the process and see what happens if she does want the service but doesn't see the value.

---

# ALTERNATIVE SALES CONVERSATION SCRIPT (2)

**Kobi:** Okay. Can I ask: Is it because you can't afford $5000 per month or you just don't see the value?

**Brenda:** Yes, I really want it and I can afford it but I just can't see the value.

*It's time to uncover all her objections. You need to move into the 'massive information gathering' phase of the SMASH process.*

---

## 2. Massive information gathering

Use my intelligent questions (IQ) checklist (see chapter 6) to uncover their needs and objections. You can use any of these questions to assist you in the massive information gathering phase.

# GATHERING ALL THE INFORMATION

**Kobi:** Okay. So, you want coaching, and you can afford it, but you're not sure if my service is worth the fee. Let's talk about what your goals are and what you're trying to achieve.

*In thinking about the next 12 months, what does success look like?*

*In thinking about the next 12 months, what could go wrong?*

*In thinking about the last 12 months, what went wrong?*

*etc.*

*Use my IQ checklist to uncover their needs and objections.*

**Brenda:** I want to grow my business quickly, make more profit and have an automated lead generation system that fills the sales pipeline and gives me predictable cash flow.

**Kobi:** Fantastic. What else would you like to achieve?

*Keep asking the IQ questions.*

**Brenda:** I want a scalable, repeatable recruitment process that enables me to hire more people so that I can get off the tools and work on the business and prepare it for sale.

**Kobi:** And what else?

*Keep asking the IQ questions.*

**Brenda:** I want to be able to take a holiday knowing that the work will be done to my standard so that I don't have to worry or get complaints from clients while I am away.

**Kobi:** And what else?

You can cycle back through these questions as often as needed to flush out every objection the prospect has. Be curious, ask open-ended questions, ask them what they're thinking, what's on their mind, what else, and so on. They need to get everything off their chest before you jump in with a solution.

## 3. Acknowledge their responses

At every stage of the selling process, you need to demonstrate that you have heard what they have said by acknowledging their answers to your questions. This can take the form of a simple, 'I see', 'Right' or 'Awesome', or you can paraphrase key words and sentences. Don't be afraid to paraphrase or repeat back the exact or similar words to those the prospect gives you. Trust me. They won't say, 'Why are you repeating what I just said back to me?' People love hearing their words reflected at them. It makes them feel heard and understood.

It's all about using verbal and non-verbal language to build rapport and make them feel heard. Good salespeople are emotionally aware and are always on the lookout for signs of distress or interest.

---

## ACKNOWLEDGING THE PROSPECT'S ANSWERS

**Kobi:** Okay. Great. So, from what I've heard, Brenda, you want to grow your business, make more profit, create an automated lead generation process so you can fill the pipeline and better predict cash flow.

*Paraphrase what they just said.*

Am I on the right track?

*Check in to get a 'yes'.*

**Brenda:** Yes, that's exactly what I want.

**Kobi:** You want to have a system for hiring more staff so that you can reduce your time on site and spend more time working on the business and prepare it for a future sale.

*Paraphrase what they just said.*

Does that sound right?

*Check in to get a 'yes'.*

**Brenda:** Yes, that's exactly what I want.

**Kobi:** You want to be able to take a holiday knowing that the work will be done to your standard so that you don't have to worry or get complaints from clients while you are away.

*Paraphrase what they just said.*

Does that feel right?

*Check in to get a 'yes'.*

**Brenda:** Oh yes, Kobi. You've read my mind! That's exactly what I want.

*Paraphrasing helps the client feel you have listened to them. It builds trust and rapport. Now it's time to move to the next step.*

## 4. Showcase the service

You are now ready to present your service to your prospect. You will tailor this presentation to incorporate the information they have given you.

# PRESENTING YOUR SERVICE

**Kobi:** Okay. So that we can confirm we're on the right page, I'm going to give you a few concepts—a few ideas of how we can work together—and then you can let me know what you do and don't like.

*Foreshadow that you are about to sell them something.*

Is that okay with you?

*Check in to get a 'yes'.*

**Brenda:** Sounds good, Kobi.

**Kobi:** Excellent. So, what we're going to do is work with you on a strategic program that will empower your team members to do more, so that you can focus on the customers that are profitable and valuable.

We're going to create an automated lead generation program that runs in the background so that you don't have to worry about filling the pipeline.

And we'll set up a quality control system you can monitor remotely so that you gain the confidence to know your team are performing to the highest standards.

*You now outline your service and the benefits you offer. Frame the service using the same words they gave you.*

Am I on the right track so far?

*Check in to get a 'yes'.*

**Brenda:** Oh yes, Kobi. It sounds amazing.

**Kobi:** Great. So, when would you like to start?

*Always be closing.*

| Brenda: | I have a couple of questions first. |
| | *They are not quite ready to buy. They have some questions (also known as objections).* |
| Kobi: | Terrific. Fire away. |
| | *You need to extract every objection and overcome each one before you can close the sale.* |

## 5. Handle objections

Most objections are around:

- I don't see the value

- I don't believe you

- I don't have time for this right now

- I'm not guaranteed of an outcome.

And that's how you take a prospect from being cold to sold.

## HOW TO HANDLE OBJECTIONS

| Brenda: | I can afford this Kobi, but *I just don't see the value.* |
| Kobi: | Great. Let's talk about affordability. My goal is to 10× your investment. If you're going to be making an investment of $5000 per month, it's my goal to turn that into $50 000 per month, which is $600 000 per year, which exceeds the goal you were hoping to achieve. Would you invest $50 000 to make $600 000? |
| | *Show value and how they will 10× their investment.* |
| Brenda: | But Kobi, I've had coaches before who've told me the same thing. *I don't believe you.* |

**Kobi:** Okay, so let's go back over the process of how we're going to achieve this outcome.

We're going to be working quarterly. We're going to be looking at your financials.

And remember your goal was to double your revenue and my goal is to 10× your investment.

*Re-establish goals and outline the process you'll use to help them reach them.*

I've done it with my business, and with many of my clients' businesses, so I know how to do it and I can do it for you too.

*Insert testimonial stories as social proof and credibility that you can do what you say.*

**Brenda:** It sounds like it's going to be a lot of work and too much of a hassle. *I just don't have time for this right now.*

**Kobi:** Okay, right. So, what do you really want to be spending more time doing?

*Be curious. Find out what they want more of.*

**Brenda:** Being with my kids.

**Kobi:** That's absolutely fantastic. So, if that's your number one goal, we're going to be focusing on that. So, in order for you to spend more time with your kids each week, what is the thing you hate doing most in your business?

*Find out what they hate doing most and want to do less of.*

**Brenda:** Finances.

**Kobi:** Awesome. We're going to find the best way to help you get rid of that task. We're going to find an A-grade person or system that will unlock the potential in that part of your business because you don't enjoy doing it. When we can take that task off you, you can focus on being with your kids.

*Demonstrate how you'll help them get rid of that task.*

How does that sound?

*Check in to get a 'yes'.*

| | |
|---|---|
| **Brenda:** | Sounds great. |
| **Kobi:** | Have you got enough information to make a decision? |
| | *Always be closing.* |
| **Brenda:** | Not quite. |
| **Kobi:** | Okay. What else is on your mind? |
| | *Be curious.* |
| **Brenda:** | I am really keen Kobi, but *I don't feel that you can guarantee that outcome.* |
| **Kobi:** | I guarantee that if you follow my process, do as I recommend and commit to massive action, you will get this outcome. I offer a 100% money back guarantee so there is no risk to you. |
| | *Provide money back guarantee, testimonials and social proof.* |
| | Is there anything else on your mind? |
| | *And the process continues.* |
| **Kobi:** | Have you got enough information to make a decision? |
| | *Always be closing* |
| **Brenda:** | Yes, I have. |
| **Kobi:** | Okay. When would you like to get started? |
| | *Soft close* |
| **Brenda:** | Right now, Kobi. |
| **Kobi:** | I'll send over the direct debit form today. |
| | *Soft close* |

## When should you quit?

At any point in this process, did you think, 'Kobi! Give it up! Cut her loose! She's never gonna buy!'

Sales is as much about patience as it is about persistence.

Here's the thing. Brenda might buy, but if you rush her and push her into a corner to make a decision before she's had all her objections met, she will not buy and all that effort will be expended for nothing.

Be curious. Be patient. Have empathy. Take your time.

# When should you bring up price?

Whether you're selling a pack of Tic Tac mints or a Tesla car, if the *value* of what the customer gets *exceeds the price*, they will buy, so you need to mention the ball park price as quickly as possible. Having witnessed thousands of sales presentations, I've seen that:

- rookies mention price at the *end* of the pitch
- amateurs mention price in the *middle* of the pitch
- pros mention price at the *start* of the pitch.

I often get asked, 'Kobi, why bring up the price so early? Shouldn't we let them see what they get for the price first?'

You must bring up the price quickly. You can wax lyrical about your service, but if they don't know the cost of it, they can't work out if it's good value or not. They have no context for deciphering whether it's cheap or expensive. State the price, then the benefits so they can assess the value you offer.

# What great salespeople do

Don't wait for the end of the sales conversation to close the deal. Great salespeople follow the ABC method: Always Be Closing. Here's a host of other soft close scripts you can use:

- Have you got enough information to make a decision?
- When would you like to make this happen?

- Is there anyone else you need to confer with to make this decision?

- Can I get you my bank details so that we can process the deposit?

- When would you like to transact?

- Would it be okay if we filled out a direct debit form?

## How to deal with tyre kickers

Do you ever get asked, 'Can I buy you a cup of coffee? I'd like to pick your brain on something.'

I get this all the time and I bet you do too. This is how the conversation plays out:

**Brenda:** Hey Kobi, thanks for all that information in your proposal. Look, before I make a decision, would you have half an hour for a coffee so I can pick your brain? I live locally. I could really do with some advice.

**Kobi:** Let me ask this, Brenda. On a scale of 1 to 10, how close are you to saying 'yes'?

If she's close to saying yes, cycle back into the SMASH process and elicit her objections.

If she can't make a decision, ask her, 'What further information do you need to make this happen?' This will weed out any lingering objections.

If she is nowhere near ready to buy, put her on the database, give her access to your free resources and keep her as a warm prospect. If she still asks for free advice, say:

**Kobi:** Brenda, I'm sorry, but I can't. My time is valuable. I have to put food on the table for my family. You can have access to all my free resources online, but if you want to work with me personally, we need to have an exchange of value.

It's only fair.

## You are not selling. You are being of service

Selling is hard. It brings up all sorts of fears. But if you take a moment to remember 'why' you are in business, and your purpose, you can easily move past those limiting beliefs and focus on how you're going to *help* them, rather than focus on how you're going to *sell* to them.

I love coaching because I sincerely believe that I can protect business owners from making poor decisions that could send them broke. I haven't forgotten what it feels like to lose your home and be on the streets. I don't want any family to go through what we did and if I can help a family avoid that, I will.

I wish I had met someone like me back in 2012. If someone had cared enough to ask me these kinds of questions when I was debating the merits of investing in a pay-per-click Google campaign—when a keyword cost 5 cents, and not $8 as it does now—my business could have been five times larger in half the time. That was the cost of inaction. I don't regret much about my business, but I regret that.

I truly believe I can help people like Brenda. She needs me and your clients need you.

As ethical entrepreneurs, we are here to serve our clients, to help them be the best they can be. To deprive them of what we offer is not only wrong, it's unethical.

# PART IV TAKEAWAYS

1. Do more. If you want massive results, you need to take massive action.

2. Don't judge the quality of your content. Let the customer make up their own mind.

3. Post content with no expectation of a return.

4. Don't measure your success based on the results of one post.

5. Pay to find the best mentors. If you don't have skin in the game, you won't make changes.

6. If your instinct tells you to do something, pay attention. Don't ignore it.

7. Always ask, 'What does the five-star version of this situation look like?' and then work hard to offer it.

8. You don't need a big budget to offer five-star service.

9. If you don't know how to resolve a customer conflict, ask them what they need to see/feel in order to feel satisfied.

10. If you can't sell, learn how to. Those who can't sell are doomed to fail.

11. Mention price early in the sales call and then explain what they get for their money.

# PART V

# MONEY

Τhis is the section you've been waiting for. You'll discover the answers to all the questions you've ever had about how to buy and sell a business. How do you find the buyers? How can they find you? What's your business worth? How do you value it? How can you maximise its value before you sell? It's not what you think it's worth, of course. It's what others think it's worth. Discover how buyers think, how they calculate value and the due diligence they undertake to assess your worth.

Novice sellers make rookie errors that can diminish the sale price by millions. These mistakes are easily avoidable. Discover what they are so that you don't make them.

What are the metrics that really matter and what are the top 21 key drivers of business value that buyers look for? If you've ever wondered how multiples work and how they are used to value a business, chapter 24 will be of value. How do they really work, can they be manipulated, what are the industry benchmarks by which you'll be valued and how can you increase the multiples used to value your business?

You'll learn why dashboards are critical to success, the top 15 dashboards you need to install, what to measure and what not to worry about. And believe it not, there's a quick and easy way to dramatically increase profit literally overnight. Few have the courage to implement it. Do you? It's easier than you think.

*Act as if* you're going to sell the business from the minute you begin it.

# Chapter 24
# The top 21 metrics business buyers look for

**M**ost entrepreneurs *begin* a business without much thought as to how they will *end* the business. They also tend to build a business around their technical skill: hairdressers open hair salons, builders start construction companies, chefs open restaurants. The trouble is, these technicians get so involved in 'doing the work' that they don't stop to think about what they really want from the business, or what they want the business to do for them.

Fast forward five, ten or 15 years, and the business owner starts to think, 'I'm tired and a bit bored. I wouldn't mind moving on or doing something different. Maybe I should sell the business?' They then work backwards to find out what they should have done at the start.

Here's a thought: why not start with the end in mind and *act as if* you're going to sell the business from the minute you begin it? If you do, I can assure you that you'll do things very differently and you'll end up with a much more valuable asset in half the time.

I didn't do this. I started my business when I was 29 years old, and wasted a good ten years working out what I wanted the business to do for me and why I was in business to start with. Now I know differently and I want to share that hard-won wisdom with you so you can get to where you're going more quickly.

If you truly want to sell your business, it pays to know what buyers look for *before* you even start your business: *before* you spend too much money, hire too many staff or make too many decisions.

You also need to think like a business buyer. If you were buying a business, what would you look for? Write that down and use that as a guideline for how you'll build your business.

If you want to build a business others want to buy, you need to get educated *now* about what a buyer looks for when assessing a potential acquisition. Getting this right now will enable you to sell the business for a much higher fee later on.

# What buyers look for when they buy a business

Buyers don't just look at what your *current results* are today. They want to know what your *potential results* are going to be too. They also want to know what's working, what's not, how to grow profits into the future, avoid preventable catastrophes and create a robust balance of risk vs reward.

## Top 21 growth metrics

Here are the top 21 growth metrics that give buyers a holistic picture of how successful you are *now*, and how likely you are to be successful in the *future*. They are divided into measurable factors and non-measurable factors and will vary depending on the business or sector you are in.

- *Measurable factors:*
  1. Net profit
  2. Asset turnover
  3. Strike rate
  4. Annual contract value (ACV)
  5. Monthly recurring revenue (MRR)
  6. Average revenue per customer
  7. Customer churn (CC)
  8. Churn rate
  9. Customer retention rate
  10. Customer acquisition cost (CAC)
  11. Customer lifetime value (CLV)
  12. Lead to Customer Conversion Rate (Recurring Customer Conversion rate)
  13. Net promoter score (NPS)
- *Non-measurable factors:*
  14. Intellectual property (IP)
  15. Marketing attractiveness and growth
  16. Customer concentration
  17. Competitive advantage
  18. Owner dependency
  19. Sales processes
  20. Management team maturity
  21. Knowledge management and retention.

Following is a brief overview and an example of what each metric means and how it is calculated.

## 1. NET PROFIT

Net profit is basically the amount of money you have left over after you subtract all your expenses from your total revenue. So, it's like the money you get to keep for yourself or for your business to reinvest. Think of it like your pay cheque after your bills are paid—it's what's left in your bank account. Net profit is the figure you really need to pay attention to. It's what makes you successful, and it's what buyers look for. All they care about is, will this investment make them money?

*The calculation looks like this:*

Net profit = gross profit (*or total income*) – all expenses

*Example:*

Your pottery business sells $20 000 worth of handmade plates per year. It costs you $11 000 in clay, paint, labour (your time) and studio hire to make them, and you pay $4000 in tax to the government.

*Result:*

$20 000 – $11 000 – $4000 = $5000 net profit

To calculate the ratio, you need to divide net profit by sales and multiply by 100 to get the percentage:

$5000 / $20 000 × 100 = 25%

*To make your business attractive to a prospective buyer:*

This figure needs to be greater than 20%. As a rule of thumb, magic happens when you hit the $1 million profit mark. It is a leading indicator that attracts the attention of potential buyers and gives you the energy and confidence to take more risks.

## 2. ASSET TURNOVER

This metric measures the ratio between the revenue you make and the costs of holding the asset that generates that revenue. In simple terms, it means how much revenue you earn based on the assets you have. We want this figure to be high because it means the asset is being used efficiently.

*The calculation looks like this:*

Asset turnover = total revenue / total assets

*Example:*

You run a crane hire business. Your revenue is $2 000 000 per year. The cost to buy/maintain your crane is $400 000.

*Result:*

$2 000 000 / $400 000 = 5%

*To make your business attractive to a prospective buyer:*

This figure should be greater than 5%.

## 3. STRIKE RATE

The strike rate is calculated by dividing the total number of sales by the total number of opportunities to make a sale. For example, how many prospects do you need to talk to in order to win X amount of business?

*The calculation looks like this:*

Strike rate = (enquiries or leads / number of sales) × 100

*Example:*

You run an air-conditioning installation business. Four prospects requested a quote. One of those four signed up to your service.

Strike rate = (1/4) × 100

*Result:*

Strike rate for your milestone = 25%

*To make your business attractive to a prospective buyer:*

This figure should be greater than 25%.

## 4. ANNUAL CONTRACT VALUE (ACV)

This metric tells you about the revenue an investment has generated over a period of 12 months with regard to the capital invested in it. It's also known as return on investment (ROI).

*The calculation looks like this:*

Annual contract value = [(present total value of investment – initial value of investment) / initial value of investment] × 100

*Example:*

You are an accountant and you sign up clients who pay you an average of $10 000 per year. You sign up lots of new clients.

Total annual contracted value = [($125 000 – $100 000) / $100 000] × 100

*Result:*

Total annual contracted revenue needs to be increasing year on year.

*To make your business attractive to a prospective buyer:*

This figure should be greater than 25% year on year.

### 5. MONTHLY RECURRING REVENUE (MRR)

This metric tells us about the earnings that a company generates every month and identifies the likely income stream that will be generated in the future.

This metric is the holy grail for those looking to buy a business. Spotify, Netflix, Dollar Shave Club and other big subscription businesses all built their fortunes off the back of this business model. (We did too, and the buyer of our business told us it was a key metric they paid attention to.)

*The calculation looks like this:*

Monthly recurring revenue = average monthly revenue per customer × total number of accounts

*Example:*

You operate a gym and personal training studio. You have 700 clients. Each client pays you an average of $50 month to be a member.

Monthly reoccurring revenue = $50 × 700 clients

*Result:*

Monthly reoccurring revenue = $35 000

*To make your business attractive to a prospective buyer:*

This figure should be more than 8% of your total turnover.

It should also be diversified and sourced from many customers—that is, it should not be concentrated in one or a few large customers.

# HOW TO SUBSCRIPTION-IFY A HAIRDRESSING BUSINESS

You will have noticed an explosion of barber salons crop up in recent years. I don't know why it didn't happen earlier. We've all seen Trent the plumber, wearing his high-vis vest, slip surreptitiously into the women's salon, take a seat, quietly ask for a #4, bury his head in his phone and skedaddle out as quickly as he can.

So it made complete sense when Barry—the burly barber with the tatts and the big, boofy beard—set up his deluxe barber shop. With beer on tap, a pool table and a big-screen TV tuned permanently to the big-league soccer, it was no surprise Trent would choose Barry over the women's salon.

Barry is smart too. He set up a monthly subscription service whereby Trent gets a short back and sides, beard trim and a head massage for just $30 per month and pays via direct debit.

Barry the barber now has:

◆   a regular source of revenue

◆   predictable cash flow

◆   committed customers who don't need to pay each time they come in

- a chance to sell this 'ring fenced' group a host of other products and services

- no need to keep finding new customers.

A hairdresser or beauty salon could easily do the same. Women need a regular colour, cut and blow wave; they need a tan every two weeks; they need to top up their fake nails every six weeks and (maybe) get a Botox session every 12 weeks. (Of course, Botox may not fly in your neck of the woods. I live in the northern beaches of Sydney. Enough said.)

Combined, these treatment fees create a very lucrative source of revenue for the salon owner and make her business a very valuable acquisition.

## 6. AVERAGE REVENUE PER CUSTOMER

Also known as average revenue per unit, this metric quantifies how much revenue an average customer generates for a business.

*The calculation looks like this:*

Average revenue per user = total revenue generated over the fixed time period / total number of users during that period

*Example:*

You make vegan pet food and have 20 000 users. Your business generated $500 000 in revenue in 12 months.

Average revenue per user = $500 000 / 20 000

*Result:*

Average revenue per user = $25

*To make your business attractive to a prospective buyer:*

This figure should be increasing yearly.

## 7. CUSTOMER CHURN (CC)

Customer churn is a metric used to track the decrease in subscription revenue caused by customers not renewing their subscriptions.

*The calculation looks like this:*

Customer churn = [(Starting monthly recurring revenue (MRR) – ending MRR) / Starting MRR] × 100

*Example:*

You run an online magazine subscription for CEOs. You had $500000 in MRR at the beginning of a month, which dropped to $375000 by the end of the month. Your revenue churn would be:

Customer churn = [($500000 – $375000) / $500000] × 100 = 25%

*Result:*

Customer churn = 25%

*To make your business attractive to a prospective buyer:*

If you're planning to sell your business, it's essential to keep your MRR target below 10% p.a. A high revenue churn indicates that your company may be struggling to retain its customer base, which can make it less attractive to potential buyers.

## 8. CHURN RATE

Churn rate is a metric that measures the percentage of cancelled subscriptions and is similar to revenue churn. It is often an indicator of the quality of the product or the level of customer service provided. The calculation is based on the number of users at the beginning and end of a given time period. The higher this figure is, the better!

*The calculation looks like this:*

Churn rate = [(users at the beginning of a time period – users at the end of the same period) / users at the beginning of a time period] × 100

*Example:*

If a meals delivery service had 100 000 subscribers at the beginning of June and 74 000 at the end, the churn rate would be 26%.

Churn rate = [(100 000 – 74 000) / 100 000] × 100

*Result:*

Churn rate = 26%

*To make your business attractive to a prospective buyer:*

A churn rate of less than 10% can make your business more attractive to potential buyers.

## 9. CUSTOMER RETENTION RATE

Customer retention rate is a significant metric that measures the loyalty of your customers, and it's important to keep this figure as high as possible!

*The calculation looks like this:*

Customer retention rate = [(users at the end of a time period – users acquired during that period) / users at the beginning of a time period] × 100

*Example:*

If a wine subscription company starts September with 200 000 subscribers, gains 160 000 more during the month and ends with 350 000 subscribers, the customer retention rate can be calculated as [(350 000 – 160 000) / 200 000] × 100, which results in a retention rate of 95%.

Customer retention rate = [(350 000 – 160 000) / 200 000] × 100

*Result:*

Customer retention rate = 95%

*To make your business attractive to a prospective buyer:*

To make your business more appealing to potential buyers, your customer retention rate should be above 95%.

## 10. CUSTOMER ACQUISITION COST (CAC)

Customer acquisition cost (CAC) refers to the expenses incurred by a business to transform a prospective buyer into a paying customer.

*The calculation looks like this:*

Customer acquisition cost = total cost incurred in marketing / total number of conversions.

*Example:*

If a make-up subscription company invests $300 000 in advertising and obtains 100 000 new customers, its CAC would be $3:

Customer acquisition cost = $300 000 / 100 000

*Result:*

Customer acquisition cost = $3 per customer

*To make your business attractive to a prospective buyer:*

In broad terms, it typically takes a year to recover the expenses associated with acquiring customers, and generally, your customers' worth should be three times the cost of obtaining them.

## 11. CUSTOMER LIFETIME VALUE (CLV)

Customer lifetime value (CLV) is a metric that determines the overall value of a customer to a business throughout their lifespan as a customer. It's a crucial metric as it enables a business to gauge a customer's loyalty and how many resources they should invest in acquiring and retaining them.

*The calculation looks like this:*

Customer lifetime value = customer annual revenue × average customer lifespan

*Example:*

If a customer spends $150 per year with you and is loyal to you for 10 years, the customer lifetime value is:

Customer lifetime value = $150 × 10

*Result:*

Customer lifetime value = $1500

*To make your business attractive to a prospective buyer:*

To make your business more attractive to potential buyers, the CLV should show a consistent upward trend every year.

## 12. LEAD TO CUSTOMER CONVERSION RATE (RECURRING CUSTOMER CONVERSION RATE)

This is an essential metric that highlights the percentage of one-time sales that are transforming into repeat customers.

*The calculation looks like this:*

Conversion rate = (total number of customers who buy again / one-off customers × 100)

*Example:*

If an insurance company gained 100 000 sales from flyers distributed at a shopping centre, and 74 000 of those sales turned into subscription customers, the conversion rate would be 74%:

Conversion rate = (74 000 / 100 000) × 100

*Result:*

Conversion rate = 74%

*To make your business attractive to a prospective buyer:*

This metric should be increasing year on year.

## 13. NET PROMOTER SCORE (NPS)

This metric is used by almost all the big corporates. It identifies how likely a customer would be to 'promote' or speak positively of your company. It's based on a customer survey and is a subjective score but investors and buyers take this metric seriously.

*The calculation looks like this:*

Net promoter score = percentage promoters – percentage detractors

*Example:*

If 90% of Telstra customers said they were 'promoters' and 10% of their customers said they were 'detractors' the net promoter score would be:

NPS = 90% – 10%

*Result:*

NPS = 80% (congratulations you are 'world class')

*To make your business attractive to a prospective buyer:*

Above 20 is great and above 50 is amazing! Check out our website (www.kobisimmat.com/guides) to download your Bonus NPS Guide to see how you measure up.

## 14. INTELLECTUAL PROPERTY (IP)

Intellectual property, or IP as it's often called, can take many forms.

For us, it's our logo on the certification stickers that all our clients display on their trucks to prove they have received certification from a trusted body.

For start-ups, it's the code that makes their software work.

For accountants, it could be their client portal.

For a coaching company, it could be their five-step training process.

For a beauty salon, it could be the exclusive right to import a special form of tanning lotion.

If you have intellectual property that is uniquely yours, and it's patented and trademarked, it creates a 'moat' that makes it hard for a competitor to copy you. It also gives the buyer of the business a strong sense of security that their unique selling proposition won't be stolen or copied. It ultimately makes your business a more valuable acquisition.

These are the nine most common types of IP rights:

1. *Patents:* these protect inventions, industrial designs and new processes

2. *Trademarks:* these protect logos, words and other branding

3. *Copyright:* this protects art, writing, music, film and computer programs

4. *Registered designs:* these protect the visual design of a product

5. *Circuit layout rights:* these protect the layout designs or plans of integrated circuits used in computer-generated designs

6. *Plant breeder's rights:* these protect the commercial rights of new plant varieties (who knew?)

7. *Trade dress rights:* these can protect the configuration of a product (e.g. Converse shoes), product packaging (the fluted Coca-Cola bottle), the interior of a restaurant (McDonald's) or colour (Louis Vuitton red-soled shoes)

8. *Geographical indications:* these rights protect words that identify a product originating from a particular place— for example, 'tequila', 'champagne', 'parmesan' or your local suburb

9. *Trade secret rights:* these rights protect the proprietary knowledge that gives a company a distinct advantage. Examples include the age-old recipe for Coca-Cola or KFC's 11 herbs and spices recipe.

# PROTECTING YOUR INTELLECTUAL PROPERTY

Unless you've got cash to burn, trying to protect your IP can be very challenging. In some cases, if you have zero budget, don't even try. It's really hard, expensive and it may not provide any protection.

Take software, for example. While it's ideal to get your software patented, for most start-ups on a budget that's a big ask as they don't have the funds to take out worldwide protection in every state, territory or country. It will also take months, if not years.

You can take out a provisional patent application (PPA) as this will allow you to file without a formal patent claim and will give you some form of protection. This will deter the amateur villains from copying your IP, but if a serious player really wanted to take your code or copy your product, they would ignore the PPA, get it to market as quickly as they could and force you to fight them in the courts. And they'd probably win because they'd have deeper pockets and could outlast you in legal fire power.

If you know you can't fight off a predatory offender, the best strategy to employ is the 'speed to market' option—that is, get the product into the hands of customers as quickly as possible, build your database, create loyalty and goodwill, publish a reputable book that showcases your process, build the brand and get that 'first mover' advantage. That's all you can do. It's also the *best* thing to do because at some point you have to sell your product so you may as well get started and use the threat of predatory copycats as the 'fire in the belly' to get the process started. Like most things in business, speed is the key to success.

## 15. MARKET ATTRACTIVENESS AND GROWTH

If you were a gambling person, would you bet that your industry is on the incline or the decline? Can you see the sector expanding or contracting?

Think tobacco.

Is it growing or declining?

Coal mines.

Growing or declining?

On the other hand, think vegan food products, pet care products, ethical investments and solar power. All are on the upswing. They have a high level of 'market attractiveness'.

If you can choose the business you want to be in, choose a dynamic, exciting sector that is on the incline, has huge growth potential and is on the right side of the ethical equation. It's important to remember: if one wants to be acknowledged as a successful business person, then one must first choose to go into a successful business.

From a market growth perspective, is there potential to move into new market segments? Does it have global potential? Could you expand vertically or horizontally? Think big from the start and reach for the sun. If you fall short, at least you'll land among the stars.

## 16. CUSTOMER CONCENTRATION

If you sell pasta, potatoes or toilet paper and you have Woolworths or Coles as your one and only customer, that's called 'customer concentration'. That's dangerous, high risk and decidedly unattractive to a potential buyer. One change of management, one downturn, one cheaper supplier and your contract gets cancelled and you run out of business.

To cap it off, you've probably tooled up in a big way to produce the quantities these large players demand, which means your overheads and salaries are going to be substantial. It also means you will have almost zero bargaining power. If the customer wants a cheaper price, longer payment terms, exclusivity and first pick of the product crop, you'll have two chances of pushing back: Buckley's and none. For a business buyer, this is risky.

Your goal is to spread the risk. Try to source a new supply of customers from a wide range of sectors so that if one industry falls over, or you lose one big contract, you are not left in the lurch.

## 17. COMPETITIVE ADVANTAGE

It's hard for small businesses to gain the edge over their bigger competitors, but it can be done. For example, being small gives you the opportunity to focus on niche topics. If you were a law firm, you could focus on one aspect of the law—for example, family law—become brilliant at that and build a solid reputation in this niche area.

Maybe you can create a competitive advantage by prioritising your local community. When you support your local football or netball club fundraising event, it shows your customers you care about them and where they live. Being involved at this local level demonstrates an authenticity and builds long-lasting relationships that the big corporates can't match.

Creating a competitive advantage when you don't have a big budget or market clout can be tricky, but if you're clever and innovative and think about what you can do that the others can't, you'll find something of value to offer.

If you have more practice at something, you have more experience and that gives you a competitive advantage. 'Do more' is the key!

(By the way, you don't need to look for a you-beaut, brand-new idea to be successful. Focus on a problem real people face that is not being solved well, quickly, affordably or sustainably and use that as the basis of your business.)

## 18. OWNER DEPENDENCY

This is a tough one for our technician friends. As chief maker, marketer and manager you are the key person of influence around which the entire business rotates. If you go, so does the business. If you're sick, the business stops. The business is entirely reliant on you.

I was the technician for a long time in my business. Clients would ring and say, 'I want to speak to Kobi.' If I wasn't available, clients would feel aggrieved at being 'palmed off' to a junior, or even senior, staff member. Or we'd have a big sales presentation and my team would say, 'Hey Kobi, can you present the pitch?'

Before I sold the business, I removed myself from the operational aspects and spent more time training up my team and, in particular, my senior management team. I didn't need to be there every day anyway. My dashboards told me everything I needed to know about the business: the leads coming in, the proposals going out, the conversion rate, accounts receivable, and so on. Those numbers got updated in real time and could be remotely monitored by me and anyone in the team. I could see when those metrics were moving in the wrong direction, and if they were, I could shift the levers quickly to do something about it.

A buyer of a business does not want it to be reliant on any one person, especially the owner, because it means that the proper systems, procedures and processes are not in place that enable the operation to run independently of that person.

## 19. SALES PROCESSES

Do you have a scalable, repeatable sales and marketing process? Are these systems documented and can they be turned on and off like a tap? For example, my company has a clear sales and lead generation process. It's easy to describe, each step is measurable and we can see instantly what is happening at each stage of the process so we can tweak each element as needed. Having this kind of control over your sales process ensures you have a reliable, automated system for generating leads that is not reliant on referrals, a talented sales rep or reputation.

My sales funnel is very simple but incredibly effective. I use social media and Google Ads to attract leads into my system at the top of the funnel, digital marketing to move them down the funnel and then my sales team make personal contact with them to set up 1:1 meetings and convert them into customers. Check out figure 24.1 to see what the funnel looks like.

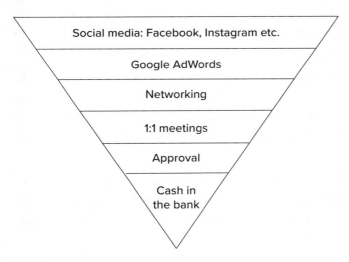

Social media: Facebook, Instagram etc.

Google AdWords

Networking

1:1 meetings

Approval

Cash in the bank

**Figure 24.1**   my sales funnel

## 20. MANAGEMENT TEAM MATURITY

A business that has a skilled and mature leadership team is always going to be valuable to a new owner. 'Maturity' in this sense is not so much about age but about experience, time in the market and the ability to lead a team. (When I was selling my business, all the prospective buyers said my management team were one of the main attractions) My team of six have been with me for many years now, are loyal and trusted lieutenants and know the business inside out. It's reassuring for a new owner to know that the team can operate independently and function without the supervision of the owner.

## 21. KNOWLEDGE MANAGEMENT AND RETENTION

I have invested significantly in our knowledge management infrastructure. All of our CRM (customer relationship management), procedures and IT systems are cloud based and driven by Google.

We started with Excel spreadsheets, moved to Google docs, then Dropbox, and then a range of customised software packages, but none of them did what we needed them to do. In the end I invested over $300 000 in building a proprietary piece of software that could 'talk' to every aspect of the business in real time. It now does exactly what we need and we've never looked back. The new owners liked that software too as they could see at a glance exactly what was going on.

This investment extended to our intranet, an essential tool in onboarding, training and performance reviews, along with maintaining our team's educational and motivational needs. And better yet, if someone leaves, their corporate knowledge does not walk out the door with them.

We've always been a cloud-based business, but this suite of software tools made us agile, fast moving and truly digital. It gave us real-time information, which meant we could make real-time decisions.

# What else a buyer looks for

What does a valuable business look like? We've covered many metrics that buyers look for. Here are a few that are not easily measured but are equally important. Make these your goals and then do the work needed to build the business.

The business needs to:

- make a profit for the current owner and future profit for the next owner
- be enjoyable to work at
- pay a fair wage for work completed

- be worthwhile continuing
- offer good value to customers
- give freedom
- give flexibility
- have a great team culture
- build wealth for you and everyone there
- leave a legacy.

Buyers of a business look carefully at these metrics because they not only shine the light on the current performance and efficiencies of the business, but they also help them identify areas for improvement once they take ownership.

It's important to remember that business buyers won't assess your business based on just one or two metrics. They'll use a large range of metrics to get a holistic picture of the health of your company. This is why it's important you understand the breadth and depth of all the metrics that the buyers will be looking at. You may not be able to 'tick the box' against all these metrics but the more you can get right, the more money you'll get for your business.

## The power of the dashboard: what we measure

You know the old saying, 'You can't manage what you can't measure.' It's a cliché, but it's true, which is why we measure everything. I was committed to this endeavour from the day I started Simmat and Associates and set up the most basic Excel-based dashboard to keep track of my team while I traipsed through South America.

That dashboard has evolved dramatically, but the seeds of that system were sown many years ago and I am reaping the rewards of that decision now.

For example, when COVID-19 hit, and everyone was instructed to work from home, we were able to flick the switch and everyone was up and running from home within hours. Hybrid working is here to stay so we are well placed now and into the future for whatever happens. I can be anywhere—on my boat, in the Daintree Forest or in the Sahara Desert—and with one click on my dashboard, I know exactly what is going on.

You might be asking, 'What metrics should we measure?' In a word, everything. In addition to the 21 growth metrics that business buyers look for, here's what else we measure on a daily basis. Your metrics will be different, of course, but you can gain inspiration from what we measure and adapt it to suit your business.

## What we measure

We break down the metrics into five categories:

1. *Finance:*
   - Cash spent and cash collected
   - Cash position
   - Percentage of debtors at 60 and 90 days

2. *Marketing:*
   - Number of posts
   - Value of quotes sent
   - Number of qualified leads

3. *Sales:*
   - Percentage of proposals won
   - New sales invoiced
   - New clients >$50000 p.a.

4. *Talent and human performance:*
   - Results of internal culture survey
   - Number of suggestions implemented
   - Number of hours of staff training delivered per month

5. *Service delivery:*

- Number of reports with a due date over two days
- Number of clients not certified within six months
- Number of clients lost.

Figure 24.2 illustrates exactly what our dashboards look like and what they measure.

You'll notice most of our dashboards have a dotted line. This is our target. If the column exceeds that, we know we are ahead of the game. Below it, there is work to do. Our monthly dashboards are easy to read, simple to understand and highly visual. One glance and you can see what's going on.

Data is everything. Without it, it's impossible to make fact-based decisions. It means you have to rely on your gut instinct. When you have a large team and many clients, that's not possible or desirable. Metrics take the guesswork out of hiring and firing; give us a strong leg to stand on if a person is not performing; and help the team understand what I value, look for and reward.

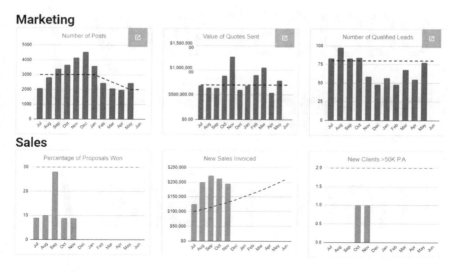

**Figure 24.2** Simmat and Associates' dashboard

Put your prices up. It's the fastest, easiest way to make more money.

# Chapter 25
# How to make (a lot) more money

**W**ant to make more money? Put your prices up.

It's the fastest, easiest way to make more money. I know you're afraid to put your prices up. You're scared you'll lose customers. But think about it this way: if you doubled your prices, would you lose half your customers?

## What does value really mean?

Oscar Wilde once said, 'A fool is someone who knows the price of everything and the value of nothing'.

I found this out the hard way.

Have you ever bought cheap garbage bags? I have. Bad decision. I hoisted the bag out of the rubbish bin; it split its side and dumped its juicy contents all over my nice clean carpet. The bag cost me $1, but it cost me $300 to get the nice guys from Electrodry to clean up the mess.

Pricing is inextricably linked to value. We focus way too much on the price of things without thinking about the value we offer in return. Most people struggle to remember the price of what they purchased even just a few hours after they've bought it. Pricing is one of the most neglected area of marketing, yet it is the easiest lever to pull and can have the biggest impact.

Write this on a post-it note and pin it up on your wall:

*When value exceeds price the clients will flow.*

If we can demonstrate value, price becomes irrelevant. Buying becomes a 'no-brainer'.

## Price vs value

I recall meeting my business coach for the first time at a local café. He said, 'What's on your mind?' I spent five minutes telling him what was bothering me. He then spent five minutes telling me the solution to my problem.

The next day, he sent me a bill for $4000.

I was aghast. Surely this couldn't be right? For 10 minutes of work?

I called him up. 'Don't you think that's a bit much for 10 minutes of work?' I asked.

'Kobi, it's like this,' he explained. 'Any standard business coach would have taken at least three sessions to answer that question, and it would have been a sub-optimal answer. It took me five minutes to understand your problem and five minutes to come up with a solution. Put my advice into practice. If it works, you pay my bill. If it's doesn't, don't.'

My $4000 investment saved me $100 000. It was a no-brainer.

He has been my business coach ever since.

# Three profit drivers

Revenue is the result of price and volume. Profit is the difference between revenue and cost. This means that every business has only three profit drivers:

- *Cost:* If times are tough and people aren't buying, the owner gets obsessed with cost cutting or 'improving efficiencies'. As such, the first lever an owner pulls is the 'cost' lever. They cancel marketing campaigns, stop buying birthday presents for the team and cut the car allowances.

- *Volume:* The second 'easiest' lever to pull is 'volume'. For example, the factory sends the sales team home early to cut wages, or they shut the factory down for a day each week to minimise overheads (both of which drive down the need for more volume). They sell more at a discounted rate, or they invoke their sales team to sell more and create new or innovative ways to drive unit sales up.

- *Price:* The last lever is 'price' and it's rarely used as a tool for generating more profit, but as a race to the bottom to see who can offer the cheapest price. This results in a price war and the only one who wins that battle is the customer.

All of these profit drivers are important, but they affect profit to different degrees. The irony is that the prioritisation owners place on each factor is in inverse proportion to the impact these drivers have on profits.

In other words, price often gets the least attention, but has the greatest impact.

# A small price rise can make a big difference

Don't take my word for it. Let's look at a real-life situation and see what happens to profit when we adjust the three variables of cost, volume and price.

ABC Pty Ltd make power drills. They manufacture them in their local factory and distribute them to Bunnings, Mitre-10 and other hardware stores. Let's play with these three variables to see which has the biggest impact on profit.

- *Scenario 1 (the control group):*
  - » Wholesale price: $100 per drill
  - » Unit sales per year: 1 million
  - » Revenue per year: $100 million
  - » Cost of goods: $60 per drill
  - » Fixed costs: $30 million
  - » Total costs: $60 million ($60 × 1 million sales) + $30 million = $90 million
  - » Profit per year: $10 million
  - » Profit margin: 10%

Let's see what the impact on profit becomes if we play with each variable by just 5 per cent.

- *Scenario 2 (increasing the price by 5%):*
  - » Wholesale price: $105 per drill (up from $100)
  - » Unit sales per year: 1 million
  - » Revenue per year: $105 million (up from $100 million)
  - » Cost of goods: $60 per drill
  - » Fixed costs: $30 million
  - » Total costs: $60 million ($60 × 1 million sales) + $30 million = $90 million
  - » Profit per year: $15 million (up from $10 million)
  - » Profit margin: 15% (up 50% from 10%)
- *Scenario 3 (increasing the volume by 5%):*
  - » Wholesale price: $100 per drill

» Unit sales per year: 1 050 000

» Revenue per year: $105 million

» Cost of goods: $60 per drill

» Fixed costs: $30 million

» Total costs: $63 million ($60 × 1 050 000 million sales) + $30 million = $93 million

» Profit per year: $12 million

» Profit margin: 11.4%

- *Scenario 4 (reducing the* variable costs *by 5%):* the profit improvement would be 30 per cent

- *Scenario 5 (reducing the fixed costs by 5%):* the profit improvement would be 15 per cent.

Figure 25.1 provides a visual representation of how drivers affect profit.

## Leverage of profit drivers

**If the profit driver improves by 5%**      **Profit changes by**

| If the profit driver improves by 5% | Profit changes by |
|---|---|
| Price | 50% |
| Variable unit costs | 30% |
| Sales volume | 20% |
| Fixed costs | 15% |

**Figure 25.1**    how drivers affect profit

It's clear that any improvement of these three drivers delivers a significant impact on profit, but improving *prices* has the greatest impact. If you want to make more money, put your prices up. Someone has to be the most expensive. Why not you?

# Establish a fair price for the business

# Chapter 26

# How to accurately value your business and get the highest sale price

I f you're selling your business, the first question on a prospective buyer's mind is the business's worth. Similarly, if you were looking to purchase a business, you'd want to determine its value. Valuation is a complex process that involves assessing several variables, and there are various approaches to determine a business's worth.

To begin, it's essential to establish a fair price for the business based on objective data rather than subjective estimates. Instead of arbitrarily selecting a number, conduct a thorough analysis of the business to determine a rational valuation. The buyer needs to see value so if all the future profit opportunity is stripped out before they even buy, the deal won't take place. If you're doing the valuation yourself, make it as unbiased and accurate as possible. Inflating your numbers will only hurt you in the long run, provide an incorrect picture of your business and turn away potential buyers.

# Valuing your business

Irrespective of how you value your business, before you even think of selling, you should do the following.

## Learn how to value a business

You'll need to get familiar with the most important terms that determine the value of a business. For example, one of the most important terms you should look into are seller's discretionary earnings (SDE) and earnings before interest, taxes, depreciation and amortization (EBITDA).

SDE and EBITDA are arguably the two most common types of business valuation methods. They're similar but different. Both are used to calculate a business's pure net profits, with SDE most often used for small businesses under $500 000 in value, and EBITDA for businesses above that.

### WHAT IS THE MEANING OF SDE, AND HOW CAN IT BE CALCULATED?

SDE, or seller's discretionary earnings, is a financial metric used to ascertain a small business owner's genuine historical profit. Computing SDE standardises or 'normalises' a business's earnings, making it easier to compare with other companies and the industry overall.

SDE can be calculated in two ways:

- First, add back any expenses that the new owner will not have to incur on an ongoing basis to net income.

- Second, subtract any expenses that will be required to maintain the business's existing SDE from gross profit. The most obvious expenses that will carry over to the new owner are advertising and non-owner salaries or contractor wages.

For instance, if a business was sold for $2 400 000, and its SDE was $700 000, the SDE multiple would be 3.42. Therefore, if the SDE of a business similar to this was $900 000, the business's worth could be estimated at around $3 000 000:

$$\$900\,000 \times 3.42 = \$3\,078\,000$$

Once the accurate earnings of a business are calculated through SDE, it can be compared with other comparable businesses that have been previously sold.

### WHAT DISTINGUISHES SDE FROM EBITDA?

If you own a larger business, you may prefer using EBITDA as a valuation metric. EBITDA stands for earnings before interest, taxes, depreciation, and amortisation.

EBITDA is quite similar to SDE, but the primary difference is that EBITDA does not permit an add-back of the owner-operator's salary. Instead, the necessary salaries for running the company are included in the expenses. The reason for this is that for larger companies, it is assumed that the owners will assume more of an investor role and are not actively involved in the regular or routine business operations on a day-to-day basis.

To arrive at a fundamental calculation of your adjusted EBITDA, follow the same procedures used to calculate SDE and then, if you're the owner-operator, add in the expense of employing someone to take on your daily duties.

Remember that this figure is a market rate and may not reflect your current salary. Depending on the size of your business, in broad terms, this adjustment may range from $75 000 to more than $200 000.

## Research your industry

Buyers don't just look at your financial performance. They look at what kind of industry you are in. For example, a software company will be valued differently from a coaching company, even if the financials are fundamentally the same. Take the time to research the industry your business is in to understand its current state and direction. The value of public companies is easily found online. You can find the value of private companies on business broking or businesses for sale websites.

## Get your finances in order

Don't wait until you have a buyer knocking before you put this package together. Also, if you start early, you can take steps to improve your financial position to become more attractive. You'll need a raft of documents for the due diligence phase including:

- profit and loss statement
- tax filings
- licenses and other proprietary documents
- other basic business finance reports.

Getting your financials together is all part of the due diligence process. More on that later.

## Engage a professional valuer

A professional business appraiser will run a full financial audit of your company. Yes, you'll need to pay them but they could add a great deal to the final sale price. I did everything myself, in conjunction with my accountant, coach and lawyer, because I wanted to learn everything about the process, but that may not be something you want to do. If you can't, or don't want to, do it yourself, or hire a professional to help you.

## Review your assets

If you choose to use an asset-based valuation method, you will definitely need to make a list of all your assets. What's an asset? Anything that adds value to your business, which could be both tangible and intangible assets.

Tangible assets include:

- physical assets such as property/real estate, your production machines, and delivery vehicles
- inventory
- accounts receivable
- cash
- investments.

Intangible assets include:

- intellectual property such as patents and trademarks
- subscriber list
- brand reputation
- social media followers.

You also need to take stock of all your liabilities, which can include:

- business loans
- accounts payable
- expenses.

# What method should you use to value your business?

It's best to use multiple valuation methods to determine the value of a business, as this can provide different viewpoints and perspectives on the potential sale price. Fortunately, there are many ways to value a business. Resist the urge to blend the methods. Each method's calculation can be run separately, but merging them together may result in skewed results.

These are the five most popular approaches to valuing a business.

## 1. Income-based method

This method calculates value based primarily on income metrics such as revenue and profit. This includes the discounted cash flow method, which takes into consideration projected future cash flow value compared to risk, as well as capitalisation of earnings, which is a combination of revenue, profit and cash flow projections. This method uses metrics such as profit and revenue (typically, future projections of those metrics) as the basis for valuation.

There are two primary methods used within this income approach 'bucket': the capitalisation of earnings method and the discounted cash flow method.

### CAPITALISATION OF EARNINGS METHOD

This method takes into account factors such as a business's cash flow to calculate its future profitability. This method is best for established businesses with stable profit.

### DISCOUNTED CASH FLOW METHOD

This method, which calculates the value of a business based on its future cash flow projection, is ideal for new businesses with high growth potential.

# HOW TO USE THE INCOME-BASED METHOD TO PROPERLY VALUE YOUR BUSINESS

Liz owns a café in the bayside suburb of Brighton. She wants to sell it, realise its value and move to the mountains to retire. It's valued at less than $500 000 so we'll use the SDE method to value it.

Here's her basic financial data:

Annual SDE: $95 000

Annual revenue: $475 000

Real estate: $175 000

Equipment and furnishings: $35 000

Inventory: $100 000

Liabilities: $50 000

Liz will use these numbers to calculate the average value for her business.

## Calculating SDE

Using the latest statistics from benchmarking sites, the restaurant industry as a whole has an average multiplier of 1.98.

To roughly calculate the value of her business, Liz takes her $95 000 calculated SDE, found using the following formula.

Net earnings (before taxes) + personal earnings + non-essential expenses for the year (one-time, non-repeating expenses, not including COGS) – liabilities = her SDE

Then Liz runs her SDE through this equation:

SDE × multiplier (1.98)

$95 000 (SDE) × 1.98 (multiplier) = $188 100

Using this model, roughly speaking, Liz's business is valued at $188 100.

Can Liz improve the value of her business? Absolutely, and she can do so by increasing the multiple.

## 2. Asset-driven method

As the name suggests, this method uses a business's assets to calculate its value. This method is especially good for real estate and investment-based businesses. You may need to conduct further research to establish the monetary value of your assets.

## 3. Market-driven method

If you're looking for a rough guide for what your business is worth, check out the sale prices of other similar businesses in your industry. Yours may sell for a similar value. Don't just settle on the data from one sale. The more data you can provide to a potential seller, the more likely you are to convince the buyer that your figures are accurate.

## 4. Price/earnings (P/E) ratio

The P/E ratio is often used to show how much investors are willing to pay per dollar of earnings. This is obviously only relevant if the company is listed on the stock exchange. How does it work? Assume you are assessing a stock with $2 of earnings per share (EPS), which is trading at $20.

*The formula:*

Share price / earnings per share = P/E ratio

*Example:*

P/E ratio: $20 / $2 = 10

In other words, this stock has a P/E of 10, which means investors are willing to pay a multiple of 10 times the current EPS for the share.

The most common multiple used in the valuation of shares is the P/E multiple. It compares a company's market value (price) with its earnings. A company with a price or market value that is high compared to its level of earnings has a high P/E multiple. A company with a low price compared to its level of earnings has a low P/E multiple.

A P/E of 3× means a company's stock is trading at a multiple that is equal to three times its earnings.

A P/E of 7× means a company is trading at a multiple that is equal to seven times its earnings.

A company with a high P/E is considered to be overvalued. A company with a low P/E is considered to be undervalued.

Another widely used multiple is the enterprise value (EV) to EBITDA multiple, also referred to as EV/EBITDA. This multiple helps investors compare companies in the same industry or sector before making an investment decision. Many equity analysts consider EV/EBITDA to be a solid measure of 'ROI return on investment' available to potential business buyers.

## 5. Profit multiplier

The profit multiplier method is a common way to assess the value of a business. Prospective buyers are often interested in the income they can earn from a business, which is why this method uses earnings as the basis for determining a business's value. However, other factors and variables are also taken into account to determine the attractiveness of the business.

To use this method, two figures are needed: the first is the business's average annual net income or profit. While the previous year's profit can be used, it may not be a reliable estimate due to various factors.

(*Note*: My buyer tried to use my last year in business as the estimate. It was not a great year for us. I negotiated with them to use the last three years as the estimate. This made a big difference to the ultimate price they paid for us.)

The second figure is an industry standard or multiple commonly applied by businesses in the same industry. If a company had an unusually large profit in the previous year, which could mean they make less profit in the following year, the profit multiplier method may result in an overly strong valuation that does not truly represent the value of the company.

Therefore, it's essential to consider average profit over a more extended period—such as three to five years—to avoid any inconsistencies.

## SO WHAT EXACTLY IS A MULTIPLE?

What exactly does the term 'multiple' mean? It is a number used in the profit multiplier approach to assess the value of businesses within the same industry.

The multiple figure varies depending on the industry, with Liz's café example indicating a multiplier of around 2 for food service businesses. This means that to determine the value of a business, you multiply its profit by 2.

The multiple figure is not fixed and may vary annually depending on various factors and trends that affect the industry.

Investors use multiples to identify a company's growth, productivity, and efficiency. A multiple measures aspects of a company's financial wellbeing or performance. It is determined by dividing one metric by another metric. Experienced business buyers and investors can look at just a few numbers and know if a business is worth buying.

The multiplying factor is negotiable. That phrase is probably the most important message I want to communicate. *The multiplying factor is negotiable!* The question is, who sets it and how can you increase it?

The answer? You set it, in conjunction with the buyer, but you need to give them good reasons why you think the multiple should be higher than what they think it should be. How do you get the multiple higher? You do all the things I have outlined in this book, but in particular, use the 21 metrics listed in chapter 24 as a guideline for how to increase the multiple.

For example, if you have a:

- steady, long-term, mature management team, you can increase the multiple

- low customer concentration (e.g. lots of different customers in different sectors), you can increase the multiple

- year-on-year increase in profit, and the projection looks set to continue, you can increase the multiple

- subscription-based revenue model, you can increase the multiple

- scaleable, repeatable source of lead generation, you can increase the multiple.

Look at each of the 21 metrics and see if you can make those metrics work in your favour. If so, you'll be able to value your business using a higher multiple.

### INDUSTRY MULTIPLIERS

Table 26.1 sets out a rough estimate of the industry multipliers for a range of sectors. Note that e-commerce is valued differently. Many of them don't show a profit for many years, so they are assessed on revenue.

**Table 26.1** industry multipliers for a range of sectors

| Sector | EBITDA multiple range |
|---|---|
| Financial | 7–12× |
| Food processing | 5–10× |
| Waste and industrial | 4–10× |
| Education | 5–12× |
| IT and digital | 6–14× |
| Energy, power and utilities | 6–10× |
| Transport and logistics | 5–10× |
| Healthcare | 6–14× |
| Tourism | 5–12× |
| e-commerce | 0.75–3×* (represents EV**/sales) |
| Professional services | 5–12× |

* e-commerce businesses are generally valued using a revenue multiple
** EV: enterprise value

# HOW MY BUSINESS WAS VALUED

We made an average profit of $1 million in the last three years I had the business. We used the multiple of 20 to value the business, which meant, roughly speaking, my company was valued at $20 million (i.e. $1 million × 20 (multiple) = $20 million.

We were able to claim an above-industry average multiple as we had nailed so many of the 21 metrics listed earlier.

There's a lot to consider here. For a technician not used to dealing with numbers, this may get overwhelming, so consider hiring a professional appraiser.

It's your business. You worked hard to grow it into what it is today, so don't skip this important step of valuing your own business. You want to get the highest possible valuation. Take the time to do the work so you are well prepared when that buyer comes knocking.

There is no one 'right' way to sell your business or attract a buyer.

# Chapter 27
# How to find a buyer for your business

N ow that you know what the business is valued at, it's time to find a buyer. There is no one 'right' way to sell your business or attract a buyer.

## Finding an interested buyer

Here are the top five ways to find a buyer for your business.

### 1.  Ask your accountant, banker or lawyer

If you have a good relationship with your advisors, ask them to send out a note to their database letting them know your business is on the market.

A note from a reputable, third-party authority goes a long way to creating trust and letting the potential buyer know that your business is a legitimate operation and worthy of consideration.

Chances are your buyer will need finance to fund the purchase. Your banker/financial advisor may have clients on their books who are looking for an acquisition. They will be incentivised to make that introduction as they will potentially win business by referring you to their client.

When you choose the accountant or lawyer to step you through this important transaction, ensure they have experience on both sides of the table in that they should have represented buyers as well as sellers. If you do find a buyer, you'll work closely with your advisors to bring the deal to fruition, so bring them into the tent as early as possible and get their advice and support.

## 2. Contact a buyer's agent or broker

There are many agents and brokers who claim to have hundreds (or thousands) of buyers ready to do business. By all means, investigate these services and explore their offering. Many are very good at what they do, will step you through the entire process, help you get your documents in order, introduce you to buyers and negotiate the sale. Do your research, interview them, ask for references and review their success stories.

Many offer a free 'discovery call' service to help you determine the value of your business. Book a call, listen for the questions they ask and that will also indicate what your buyers look for in a new acquisition.

## 3. List it on a website

There are lots of 'businesses for sale' websites. Most are in the business of selling retail style—that is, bricks and mortar operations—but there are some dedicated to selling in a specific niche that may match your needs. You need to reveal some financials to the public to make this method viable but it is an easy way to promote the sale and find potential buyers.

## 4. Seek a trade sale

A trade sale is when you sell your company, or part of it, to another business that will carry on the company's trade. The acquiring company, known as the trade buyer, works with the acquired company (or the trade seller) to make sure that all the terms of the sale go smoothly. You may not need to look too far afield to find a trade buyer. It could be one of the following.

### COMPETITORS

Competitors are prime targets as they may want to grow their business, expand their operations or take on a new product. Rather than do it all themselves, it can be easier and quicker to buy a competitor.

For example, if you own a bakery and sell to a competitive bakery, they get all your equipment, database, leases, goodwill, and more. This is a fast way for them to increase the size and scale of their business without needing to build it from the ground up again.

You could also consider selling part of your business to a competitor: hold onto the part you love doing and dispose of the part you don't.

This strategy is called a 'horizontal' integration. There are several benefits associated with this strategy. The business:

- gains a larger customer base
- increases revenue
- cuts out the competition
- creates synergy between two companies (including marketing resources)
- reduces production costs.

Think about what you have and how valuable you would be to a competitor. When you are ready, reach out to ask for a chat or ask your accountant to broker the meeting.

## SUPPLIERS

You may have a supplier (or distributor) interested in expanding their operations. Take the bakery for example. Maybe their oven manufacturer or the coffee supplier wants to open a retail operation. Rather than start from scratch, they may look to buy an ongoing concern to save time and effort. This strategy is known as vertical integration. There are a number of benefits associated with vertical integration. The business:

- streamlines operations

- reduces production costs

- captures upstream or downstream profits

- accesses new distribution channels

- cuts down delays in delivery and transport.

Have a think about all the suppliers you do business with. Could one benefit from acquiring you?

Companies can also integrate vertically by moving backwards or forwards:

- *Backward integration:* This is when a company buys another business that makes an input product for the acquiring company's product. For example, a backward integration for a bakery would be if they bought a flour mill that produced the flour for making bread.

- *Forward integration:* This is when a company buys another business to take control of the post-production process. For the bakery, it might mean they buy a series of restaurants that serve their bread or baked goods as part of their menu.

## CUSTOMERS

Don't ignore those you currently do business with as potential buyers. They already do business with you, and know and (hopefully) love what you do. They may be looking for a new opportunity, lifestyle or challenge. You can advertise it openly or you can be more discreet and target certain individuals and check out their interest.

## 5. Social media

Your buyer is actively researching you and your competitors. How do they know who is the best? The one who is most active on social media will have a head start. Being active on social shows them who you are, what you do, why you're the best and will encourage them to put you on their list for consideration.

# Due diligence

Finding an interested buyer is one thing. Doing the due diligence is another. Be prepared. It's arduous, costly and risky. Why risky? Because you are doing a lot of legwork in putting all the documents together, showing your financials to a 'stranger' and hoping that they have good intentions. Halfway through my due diligence phase I did think, *Here I am giving them all my valuable data. What if this 'buyer' is a competitor posing as a buyer?* It had me up at night a bit. Other than check references and ask around, there is not much you can do but go along with the process in good faith and hope it works out.

When you do push the button on selling, have all your documents ready to go. That's easier said than done. But it's in your best interest to be ahead of the curve here. When my buyer emailed me asking for a range of documents, I was able to email those documents instantly because I had my house in order. This says to the buyer, 'I'm organised, I have my shit together and I mean business.' Never forget that a buyer is testing you out every step of the way. If they know it takes you three weeks to send them a profit and loss statement, they know they have the upper hand at the negotiation because they know you are not across the detail. Be ready, be prepared. You should be planning your exit at least one or two years in advance.

(If you want a full listing of what documents my buyer needed to see before sealing the deal, check out my website: kobisimmat .com/guides.

*A word of warning:* the list is onerous, but worth it. Don't be daunted. Think of the payoff. Keep the goal in mind.

## Should you hire an advisor to help you?

Yes, you should definitely involve your accountant and lawyer. Their advice will be invaluable. Having said that, I sourced most of my financial documents myself. This took me months to do, and cost me around $500 000 of my own time, but I was invested in the process, and needed to be. I plan to sell my next business so it was in my interest to know what was involved in selling this one. If you want to be a serial entrepreneur, stay close to the action, don't outsource the due diligence too much and see exactly how the process operates.

## Shit-test your assumptions

Unless you really have to sell, don't just take the first buyer who comes along. And don't assume they know what they're doing or what they're talking about. I have had many tyre-kicker buyers approach me for a meeting and after a few minutes, I could tell they didn't know as much as I thought they did. This gave me the confidence to know that I have bargaining power, I don't have to accept the first offer that comes along and I have the right to audition them as much as they are auditioning me.

You can waste a lot of time with tyre kickers. Pre-qualify them by asking these questions:

- Why do you want to buy this business?

- Do you need funding to buy this business? Have you secured that funding yet?

- Can you submit financial statements to demonstrate you can afford to fund the down-payment?

- Do you have the experience needed to run this business? If not, who will run it?

- What is your time frame for purchasing this business? Now? Six months? A year?

- Will you want me, as the current owner, to work within the business during the transition? (This is known as an earn-out.) If so, for how long and on what basis?

Although these steps may not be complicated, neglecting them can result in wasted time and resources as well as the risk of negotiating with unqualified buyers and potential leaks of confidential information before the sale.

## How should you handle these meetings?

Use my IQ checklist (see chapter 6). Take on the role of the interviewer, rather than the interviewee, and ask them all those questions through the prism of them buying the business:

- In thinking about the next 12 months, what does success look like?

- In thinking about the next 12 months, what could go wrong?

- In thinking about the past 12 months, what went wrong?

- And what do you propose to do about that?

- And what's on your mind?

- And what else?

- And if I was to be giving you some kind of help, what kind of help would you be looking for?

# How to create your information memorandum

If you're selling a business, or sourcing investors, you'll need a 'big picture' document that sums up who you are, what you do, why you're valuable and why they should buy you. This document has a few different names: an information memorandum (IM), an offering memorandum, a prospectus, a business plan and others.

In general, and this will vary depending on the type of business you are selling, the IM has the following main components:

- A non-disclosure agreement for both sides to sign

- A summary of who you are and what the business is about

- A summary of your management team

- A description of what the business owns (i.e. the asset/s)

- Profit and loss statements, a balance sheet, projected growth etc.

- An organisational chart, corporate history (with key milestones achieved) and an outline of how your company is structured

- A summary of the market, where it's heading and expansion plans, and a SWOT analysis

- The known risks that you believe the business is susceptible to (be as transparent as you can—no-one likes surprises)

- An application form or contact details for the buyer to complete to indicate their interest.

Yes, it's a lot of work to put together this document but once it is done, it's done and you can go to market quickly, put your best foot forward and attract highly qualified buyers.

# Give your staff the tools they need to do their job well.

# Chapter 28

# Don't be a tight-arse with money

L et's now shift our focus away from the inside-the-business side of business to other money matters.

I can afford any car I want. I could have a Lamborghini, a Maserati or some other fancy Italian car. But I choose to drive a Toyota LandCruiser. Why? The answer is simple. It's reliable and rarely breaks down (and it offered the lowest depreciation and yet the highest resale value). I need a car that can get me through the boggiest sand, the driest desert, the wettest forest. It's unbreakable.

Don't get me wrong. I love the exhilaration of roaring down the highway in a high-powered European vehicle, but the trouble with (most of) these extravagant cars is they break down! I can't afford to break down. Not so much financially (although that's part of it), but if I'm heading to a client meeting or heading into the outback with my family, I need to know that the vehicle I have entrusted to get me there, *will get me there*. That's why I like LandCruisers.

While it's not an expensive car in the scheme of things, my accountant and finance team tell me I can save money if I buy a cheaper car. But I have learned from bitter experience that if you want to cut corners, it will cost you in the long run. I believe in buying quality from the start and giving myself and my people the tools we need to do the job in the very best way we can.

For example, I could buy my team a Samsung phone each and save a few bucks, but those phones don't support the apps we use to run the business, and they have a short battery life. The result? If a client needs to get in touch with them quickly and my staff member is out of reach, or the network is down, or the connection is poor, my team can't do their job. They can't get the client a result and the entire relationship is jeopardised, all for a few lousy bucks. (When my clients need to get in touch with us, they need to get in touch with us *now*. It could literally be a life-and-death situation, particularly in the occupational health and safety division where a factory accident needs to be dealt with instantly.)

It's the same with computers. When I first started my business and money was tight, my IT consultant convinced me to get a cheap laptop. Within a few months, the device broke down, I lost my data, I had to hire a forensic data specialist to retrieve the files, I lost access to my computer for two days and the result was chaos. The savings made were miniscule compared to what it cost me.

For the sake of a few extra dollars per month, I give my staff the best of the best cars, computers and consumer electronics so they can do their job to the best of their ability. The long-term impact of having good-quality gear easily outweighs the short-term economic upswing.

Don't be a tight-arse with how you spend money. Give your staff the tools they need to do their job well. You get what you pay for.

Being called an 'entrepreneur' lends an air of respectability to failing.

# Chapter 29

# Why I don't like being called an entrepreneur

*E* ntrepreneur: (*n*) *a person who sets up a business or businesses, taking on financial risks in the hope of profit.*

Call me anything, but please don't call me an entrepreneur.

Back in the 1980s, the word was synonymous with being a bit slippery, slightly dodgy, an opportunist. I grew up when the likes of Alan Bond, Christopher Skase, George Herscu and other corporate rogues were having a field day fleecing the mums and dads of Australia, shuffling paper assets and running rings around the corporate regulators. Widely regarded as 'larrikin entrepreneurs', these buccaneers were lauded by the media and given access to the blue-chip boardrooms of Australia's best companies. Only later did the full fallout of their fraudulent activities become apparent.

Fortunately, there's been a shift in public sentiment to what the word 'entrepreneur' now means and those negative associations have largely subsided. Today, the word represents something entirely different. To be called an 'entrepreneur' is a compliment, a testament to your fortitude, persistence and tenacity.

On the whole, this celebration of what it means to be an entrepreneur is a good thing.

We need to teach our high school and university students the skills of entrepreneurship so they can pursue their own path, forge their identity and become independent in the pursuit of profit.

We need to teach them to rely on themselves to create their own destiny, and not rely on others or the government for a handout, or even a hand up.

We need them to start businesses without fear of failure. This entrepreneurial mindset is what keeps the economy ticking over and we need to encourage it.

## What have I got against being called an entrepreneur?

If entrepreneurship is so good and it's a quality we want to engender in our next generation of business owners, why am I personally so reluctant to be called an entrepreneur?

I don't like being called an entrepreneur because to me, the term lends an air of respectability to failing.

It lends an air of acceptability to the concept that it's okay to take other people's money and spend it on bringing a wild and crazy idea to fruition, and then, if the business does not succeed and everyone loses their money, well, that's okay too.

That tolerance for failure is not something I ascribe to. We should never go into business assuming or even contemplating it will fail.

We should definitely not go into business assuming we can use other people's money to fund our wild and crazy experiment.

The practice of using other people's money to fund a business experiment is unethical and unprincipled, but unfortunately, it's rife, and the raft of bestselling books written by the world's wealthiest about their super successful unicorn start-ups encourages it. Some people go so far as to call this style of raising capital a Ponzi scheme.

The scale-up accelerators and ecosystems responsible for training our new wave of entrepreneurs are part of the problem too. They endorse this unedifying practice (many of them have got skin in the game, so they benefit big time if the start-up goes big), and to them, losing other people's money is an acceptable, albeit inevitable, cost of doing business. Not in my book.

## What is my definition of an entrepreneur?

The difference between an entrepreneur and a wheeler-dealer needs to be called out. Wheeler-dealers take money from investors to fund a business experiment that may or may not work. There's a name for that. It's called 'fraud'. Tough language, I know, but that's what I think.

Ethical entrepreneurs take money from customers and give them what's called a product or service in return for that money. How novel. Call me old school, but in my world, building a business is all about creating a series of scalable systems, structures and procedures that enable you and your stakeholders to make a profit. It's also about empowering the next owners to make a profit (in the future) because of the work you did (in the present).

In short, an entrepreneur's mission is to see a problem, identify an opportunity, create a solution and in doing so, unlock value that exceeds the money spent in solving it. If I spend $10 and create $1000 in return, that is entrepreneurship; that is success.

Each funding choice comes with its own unique set of pressures.

# Chapter 30
# Raising start-up capital

T raditionally, there are five types of sources of funds and/ or investors. Each choice comes with its own unique set of pressures. Only you can decide which way to turn.

- *Personal investors.* Start-ups often turn to the 3Fs (family, friends and fools) to kick-start their enterprise. They are an easy source of money because they want to support their loved ones and don't want to be seen as ungenerous, short-sighted or tight-fisted. If you do take their money and lose it, which is highly probable — especially if this is your first entrepreneurial rodeo — you'll need to deal with the emotional and financial baggage that comes with that.

- *Angel investors.* Angel investors are individuals with a high net worth who provide funds in return for a share of the business, with a view to getting in early, absorbing the risk and seeing the value of their investment skyrocket. They generally fall into the 'sophisticated investor' class, know how to conduct their own due diligence and can assess deals in a detached, clear-eyed manner.

- *Venture capitalists*. These people, also known as VCs, are private equity investors. They take a stake in start-ups that exhibit high growth potential. These groups are not overly interested in seeing that start-up book a profit. They want to see demonstrable proof that the start-up has potential and value metrics such as revenue, active users, downloads and churn rate above all else, so that they can capitalise on the upside when the company goes public.

- *Banks*. Banks are a traditional source for business loans. Start-ups don't like borrowing from banks because it means the money has to be paid back (with interest) even if the enterprise folds.

- *Pre-selling to customers*. This is my preferred source of investment.

## Sophisticated investors

If you do seek investors, and need a handful to support your endeavour, an ethical approach is to target the sophisticated investor sector. The Australian Government created the term 'sophisticated investor' for a reason. They wanted to protect unsophisticated 'mum and dad' investors from being sucked into these slick sales pitches, which are often nothing more than a pyramid scheme.

For you to qualify as a sophisticated investor, your accountant needs to certify that you have had an income of $250000 per year for the past two years and that you hold net assets of at least $2.5 million. By definition, if you fall into this category, the assumption is you are fluent in financial jargon, know how to assess a deal and can make your own informed decisions. In any case, you're likely to get your accountant to check over the deal and then advise if it stacks up. Even if the accountant says 'no deal', many sophisticated investors are happy to drop half a million per deal on half a dozen founders and wait to see what happens. If only one comes good, they've more than covered their initial investment.

If you target a sophisticated investor, you do not need to provide them with the same level of product disclosure requirements that must be provided to retail ('mum and dad') style investors. Of course, it's up to every investor to do their own due diligence, caveat emptor and all that. Most sophisticated investors know what to look for, have money to burn on a super spec stock and are happy to take a risk.

## Smart vs dumb money

Let's make the distinction between smart money and dumb money. Smart money is when an entrepreneur takes money from an experienced investor who has contacts and knowledge and is prepared to put their assets to work in service to the start-up. That investor comes with their sleeves rolled up, is cognisant of the risks, knows what 'sweat equity' means and is prepared to invest in the long haul to hopefully get a 10× return on their investment.

Dumb money comes from 'mum and dad' investors, who put their money with the start-up as a 'set and forget' investment, running the risk of being burned—and it's that kind of capital raising I take exception to. That's called wheeling and dealing. You're taking money from people who don't know what they're doing, can ill afford to lose that money and will be severely impacted if the money is lost.

If you are taking money from an immature investor for a product or service just so you can increase the valuation of your business—so you can exit with a multimillion-dollar handshake and leave the investors at the end of that long conga line with a script not worth the paper it's printed on—then do not call yourself an entrepreneur because you are not. Entrepreneurs create value, help people solve a problem and provide value in excess of the price paid. If you can't do that, you're not entitled to wear the title of 'entrepreneur'—you have not earned the right. You're not allowed admittance to that club. You're not an entrepreneur—you're a wheeler-dealer.

# Big Brother

Unintended consequences can arise when you take money from investors. Take Brad as an example.

## DON'T LET GREED TIE YOU DOWN

Brad owns a manufacturing business. The business makes steel injection mouldings for the supermarket industry. Think of the chocolate bars at the supermarket checkout: he makes the metal frames that hold all those chocolate bars. It's a niche sector, he does it well and it's a good business.

He was doing well financially before he met his wife (who comes from a very wealthy family), but when he married her, he stepped into a whole new realm of wealth. A few years after getting married, Brad spotted an opportunity in the fashion sector to sell leather jackets to the rich and famous in Beverly Hills, California. Now these are no ordinary leather jackets. They are extravagantly embroidered with handmade, colourful appliqué and each is uniquely different. You could say it was a departure from his current line of work.

He couldn't fund the business himself so his father-in-law chipped in $2 million to kick it off. Brad's now got a bit of cash to play with, but he's also got a gun to his head, and his father-in-law has his finger resting heavily on the trigger. His father-in-law, once a not-so-distant relative who called before he came over to their house and kept a respectful distance to enable his progeny to proceed with her life, is now glued to Brad's boot like a piece of two-day-old gum. And Brad can't shake it. No matter which way he turns, that gum pins him to the ground. He'd love to take that shoe off so he can run fast and free, but he's stuck.

Will the jackets sell? Time will tell. Meanwhile, Brad is stuck with his father-in-law hovering over his every move. It's no way to live.

If you can't fund your business, start a business that you can fund. Start something that's super profitable. Run it, make some money and use that to support your start-up.

Here's the reality. If you take start-up capital from anyone—a family member, a mate, an angel investor, a venture capitalist or an accelerator group—you have to be prepared to live with them hanging over your shoulder like a hungry albatross, watching your every move.

Having lunch with a mate on a Friday afternoon and an investor walks by? They'll wonder why you're there and not at work.

Post a pic on Instagram having a holiday with the family at the snow? They'll wonder why you're not at work.

Picking up the kids from school? They'll wonder why you're not at work.

Wherever you go, they'll be there, waiting for their payday.

They will also have a 'to do' list for you as long as your arm and it will be *not negotiable*. There's no autonomy. They expect you to follow orders because they gave you money and they want a 10× return on it as soon as possible. It's a very stressful way to fund a business. Unfortunately, most novice business owners don't realise they're stepping into this bear pit until they're in it too deep to get out.

Don't say I didn't warn you.

I am fully aware this position is controversial and at odds with almost every business book on the shelf: *How to raise capital, How to pitch, How to scale*. They all say the same thing: go get investment.

But what they don't tell you about is the noose that comes with it. The flypaper. Whatever way you turn, those investors will be there, like Brad and his father-in-law.

# Bootstrap or die

If you want to raise capital, get it from your customers. Ask them to buy something and use the revenue raised to fund your expansion.

Or you can fund your business from private funds or through crowdsourcing. But don't take funding from investors if you want to avoid feeling like you're on borrowed time to pay them back.

I often hear young (and not so young) entrepreneurs say, 'If I take investor money and lose it, that's their problem, not mine.' That's true, of course, but what gets left unsaid is that those investors are people, with mortgages, and families, and financial commitments, and hopes and dreams just like yours, and they gave you money in good faith, in the hope that the work, sweat and effort you put in would return them a premium or dividend on that investment.

Sure, some of them are millionaires many times over and can afford to lose a buck or two without having to go without their champagne, caviar or cognac. But is that the point? Even if the loss is not felt financially, they will feel it emotionally because they believed in you and invested in you. And make no mistake, they are investing in *you*: your vision, your skill and your ability to execute a plan.

If you are aged 21 and you take money and you lose it, some will say, 'Good on you for having a crack. You have time on your side and as memories fade, you can return bigger and better—and hopefully smarter.' But people have long memories. You may forget that you lost their money, but your investors won't.

# PART V TAKEAWAYS

1.  Use the 21 metrics to identify the drivers that improve a business. Get these right, and you can substantially increase the multiples used to value your business.

2.  Build a dashboard that contains all your KPIs. It lets staff know what to aim for, keeps them accountable and makes it easy for you to quickly find out what is going wrong.

3.  Don't wait until you have a buyer knocking on your door before preparing your financial documents. Start early, and get them in order before you need them. When a buyer comes calling, you'll impress them with your responsiveness.

4.  Multiples matter, and they are negotiable. Find out what your industry multiples are and then review the 21 drivers of business value to increase the multiple used to value your business.

5.  Your accountant, lawyer, banker or coach can help you find a buyer for your business. When you're ready to sell, ask them to send out a note to their database advising that your business is up for sale.

6.  Your customer, supplier, distributor or follower could all be potential buyers. Conduct an analysis on relevant parties to establish what benefits they would derive from buying your business.

7.  Do your due diligence on buyers the way they will do due diligence on you. Shit-test their assumptions and don't assume they know more than you do about your business, the industry and what your business is worth.

8. If you want to make more money quickly, put your prices up. If you doubled your prices, would you lose half your customers?

9. When value exceeds price, the clients will flow.

10. Bootstrap or die. Try to self-fund your business from private funds, pre-sales or crowdsourced funding. The minute you take funding, you are on borrowed time to deliver a result.

11. There's never been a better time to start something new. You are the most experienced and resourceful you've ever been.

# IT'S ONLY TOO LATE IF YOU DON'T START NOW

Congratulations! You've done what most never do: finish a business book. But I'm so glad you have because now you have the recipe for how to build a business others want to buy: the step-by-step guide to moving from technician to owner and for developing the systems you need to create a profitable business that will withstand the test of time.

I have three final pieces of advice for you. I've saved them for last as they are in some ways the most important.

## Don't let the past derail your future

I have a friend, Ingrid. She's 58. She has three children aged 18, 22 and 26. They have all left home. She divorced her husband 15 years ago, dedicated her life to bringing her up children as best she could on a limited budget, and now feels bereft at their departure. She came to me seeking advice and assistance.

'What's my purpose?' she asked. 'What will I do for the next ten years? I have so much to give but I didn't have a career, I have no formal skills and I can't compete on the current job market. What do I do, Kobi?'

I said to her, 'Ingrid, at this point in your life, you are the most resilient, experienced, successful, resourceful and knowledgeable you've ever been. Take everything you've done and seen and put it into this new endeavour, whatever it may be, and use that knowledge to move on, move up or let go.'

I have a lot of people like Ingrid come to me with these kinds of regrets. They say they should have worked harder, delegated more, divorced earlier, started sooner. Coulda, woulda, shoulda.

We can all use the past as a reason for why we can't succeed in the future, but I truly believe that your chances of success right now are better than they've ever been, so just go do it! Start now.

## Focus on education *and* implementation

There's a reason YouTube is so popular. People love learning stuff. The trouble is, they don't like putting what they've learned into practice. Take Penny, for example. She's a graphic designer. She loves what she does and is good at it. She built her website, SEOd her copy, updated her LinkedIn profile, completed an advanced Canva course, got a new logo and created a pitch deck. She did all the right things but got so caught up in education, she forgot to focus on implementation.

She didn't actually send out any emails, post anything on her socials, let the world know what she was doing or why she was the best. It's a technician's curse. To know and not do is to not know. As Stephen Covey said, you're 'better off having an average strategy with superb execution than a superb strategy with poor execution'.

Ideas won't make you rich.

# Don't confuse effort with results

We all like doing certain things. Some people love analysing data. They spend hours digging into their Google Analytics to find out who landed on their page and why, or they pore over old financial records to see if everything tallies.

Some love networking. They're out at this lunch, that dinner, this conference, that forum. They love being with people, talking up their business and telling everyone how good they are.

Others prefer to connect with others online and love nothing more than making comments, Liking posts and giving advice or support.

All these activities are, in and of themselves, good things to do.

But how many of them fall into profitable activities? How many have a direct impact on the bottom line? At the end of the day, you feel you've put a lot of *effort* into the business, but did those actions generate a *result*?

Unless the work you do is part of a coordinated system that leads to a hard sale, you are working *in* the business not *on* it.

Just because you show up at work every day doesn't mean you are getting anything done.

Sometimes we get so busy caught up in effort, we forget to look at the results. So remember, activity does not always lead to accomplishment.

# THE FAST-TRACK GUIDE FOR HOW TO BUILD A BUSINESS OTHERS WANT TO SELL

Jonathan is 24 years old. He's built an app that helps schedule text messages, which is a cool idea. He's the son of a client and his father suggested he come and see me to get some advice about what Jonathan should do next.

I know what Jonathan wants me to tell him. He wants me to say, 'Get out there, think big, be bold, take the world by storm. Find some investors who will back your big idea and take as much money from them as you can and give away as little as possible in return. Use OPM (other people's money) and go hard and fast. If you fail, it doesn't matter because there will be some other schmuck ready to give you money and you can reframe that failure as a learning experience and position it as a benefit for the next investor. Don't focus on profit, focus on revenue, sales, users, downloads. Just give the investors what they want so they can sell out with a high valuation and leave the next round of mum and dad investors to pick up the pieces. Keep going until you hit that multimillion-dollar payday. Rinse and repeat.'

No, that's not what I would tell Jonathan. I would tell him to do the exact opposite. I would tell him to:

- think like an owner from the beginning
- get a pre-sale from a customer, and then another, and then another
- hire your first person as quickly as possible
- delegate everything
- think big, 10× your goals and write them down
- buy a book and note down all your goals, small and large
- surround yourself with people who are smarter than you
- read one business book a week and apply what you learn
- learn how to sell
- set the tone for your team and be stoic no matter what is happening in your life
- don't judge why people do what they do but be curious and ask why they did what they did
- invest in a dashboard and give everyone access to everyone's metrics
- give every team member specific KPIs and have weekly and monthly catchups to check on their progress
- create a cadence for communication so they know when meetings will occur
- create quarterly goals for your management team
- give your team the tools they need to succeed

- when you don't have the answer or know what to say, ask, 'what's on your mind?' and follow up with 'and what else?'

- show empathy and understanding before offering a solution

- encourage your team to take risks and don't punish them for making mistakes

- fund your growth through the sale of your products and services

- hold an annual conference and create rituals that let your team know they are valued

- appoint a board as quickly as possible and meet monthly with them

- keep good accounting records for at least four years. The new business owner will want to see them all.

## Timing is everything

As counter-intuitive as this sounds, I would also tell Jonathan that as much as I admire his youthful energy and vigour, he needs to be patient. That's not an attribute we hear a lot about these days, but I've learned over the years that if you push the universe too hard, it can push back even harder, and whack you on the side of the head. Lots of great business ideas failed because they were ahead of their time, so be patient and know that if you don't succeed, it may have been because the timing was just not right.

We can't make everything go faster. Some things just need to take their time. You can't boil an egg faster than the time it takes to boil an egg (unless you put it in the microwave and then it'll explode. I tried it). Dough needs to rise. Alcohol needs to ferment. It's the same with relationships. People need time together. Not just quality time, but quantity time.

But you can fast-track action and results by reframing the situation differently and asking better questions, and you can fast-track your success by putting into place some of the tools, tips and techniques you learned in this book.

It took me a long time to find my feet and develop the skills and confidence I have now. Don't waste time working it all out for yourself. Follow the process for building a business others want to buy outlined in the five parts of this book and you'll never have to experience the ignominy of losing your home, your reputation and your livelihood. My family and I have already paid that price so you don't have to.

I have created pathways and know where the pitfalls are, and I know that if you listen to people like me, who have been there and done that, you will get to where you want to go and do it with your financial wellbeing and reputation intact. If you want to build a business others want to buy, please implement what you have learned here and go out and make it happen. Be patient if you fail. Celebrate when you succeed. But just keep going.

You only fail if you stop.

Kind regards,

*Kobi Simmat*

There are lots of ways for us to connect:

Email: kobisimmat@gmail.com.au

Web: kobisimmat.com

TikTok: KobiSimmat

Instagram: KobiSimmat

YouTube: KobiSimmat

Download our free course: How to build a business others want to buy: www.kobisimmat.com/courses